I0605785

Letters from the Burma Front:

Dear Annie & Flo …

Letters from the Burma Front:

Dear Annie & Flo …

Kate Venables
and Harry Walker

Pen & Sword
MILITARY

First published in Great Britain in 2025 by
Pen & Sword Military
An Imprint of Pen & Sword Books Limited
Yorkshire – Philadelphia

ISBN 978 1 03610 188 6

A CIP catalogue record for this book is
available from the British Library.

Typeset by Mac Style
Printed in the UK by CPI Group (UK) Ltd, Croydon, CR0 4YY.

The Publisher's authorised representative in the EU for product safety is Authorised Rep Compliance Ltd., Ground Floor, 71 Lower Baggot Street, Dublin D02 P593, Ireland.
www.arccompliance.com

For a complete list of Pen & Sword titles please contact

PEN & SWORD BOOKS LIMITED
47 Church Street, Barnsley, South Yorkshire, S70 2AS, England
E-mail: enquiries@pen-and-sword.co.uk
Website: www.pen-and-sword.co.uk
or
PEN AND SWORD BOOKS
1950 Lawrence Road, Havertown, PA 19083, USA
E-mail: uspen-and-sword@casematepublishers.com
Website: www.penandswordbooks.com

Dedicated to Harry's grandchildren
Eloise, Matthew, Imogen and Joel,
and his great-grandchildren Freya and Zoe,
Naomi, Esme, Reuben and Rachel,
and Norah and Ishmael

Respice, Prospice

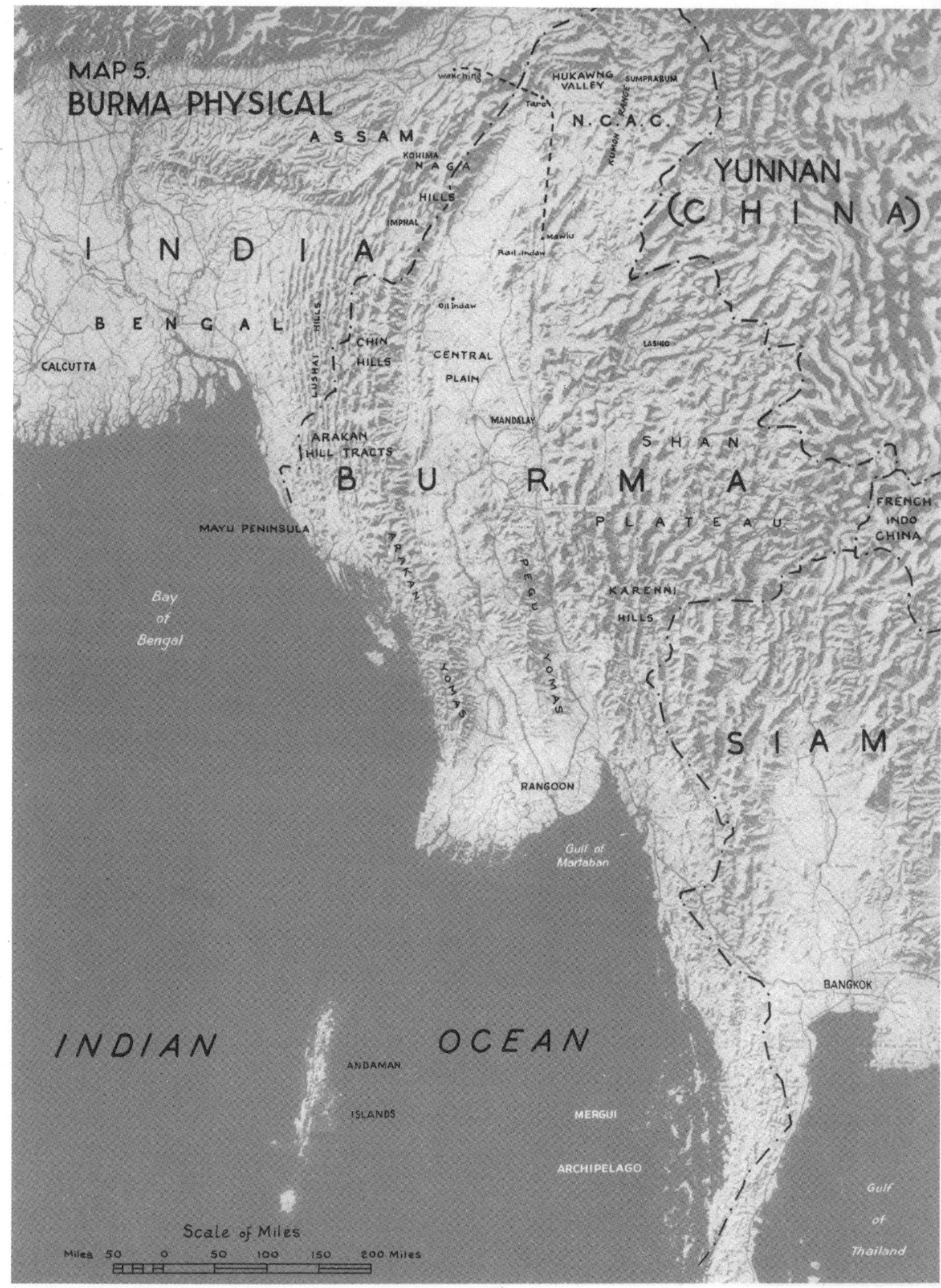

Mountbatten. *Report*, 1951.

Contents

List of Illustrations

Acknowledgements

Letters from the Burma Front: Dear Annie & Flo exists only because Harry's cousin, the late Mary Foster, retrieved the letters on which the book is based; she also saved many family photographs. It relies on archives and libraries and I thank the staff of the Bodleian Libraries, University of Oxford, the National Archives, the Imperial War Museum, the National Army Museum, the British Pathé historical collection, the Australian War Memorial, the Museum of Military Medicine, the Wellcome Library, the Burma Campaign Collection at the School of Oriental and African Studies, the Royal College of Surgeons in Edinburgh, the Royal College of Anaesthetists, the University of Edinburgh Library, the University of Liverpool Library, Teesside Central Library, the Teesside Archives and the Lancashire County Archive.

I discussed the letters with my sisters Alison Cook and Elizabeth Walker, my uncle the late Robert Walker, and my aunt the late Mary Walker. My cousins Janet Cox, Murray Foster, Susan Peel, Jean Talbutt and Barbara Wenman talked family history with me and loaned me photographs. The children of Teddy Tuller and Ben Beck, Harry's fellow medical students, allowed me to read letters and reproduce a photograph. Robert Lyman, the military historian, generously read the text and prevented a few howlers, and Penelope Gresford and Kevin Noles also offered comments. This book emerged from a larger project which draws on Harry's life and which I undertook as doctoral research at Goldsmiths, University of London. I am grateful for advice and encouragement from many staff and students at Goldsmiths. At the publisher, the book has benefitted from the professional expertise of many people, including Stephen Chumbley, Harriet Fielding, Tara Moran and Jon Wilkinson.

The letters are presented here as Harry wrote them, unedited. I have attempted to contact the friends of Harry's and family members who are named but, not surprisingly, most are now dead. I would be happy to hear of any necessary corrections. Image credits are in the figure captions.

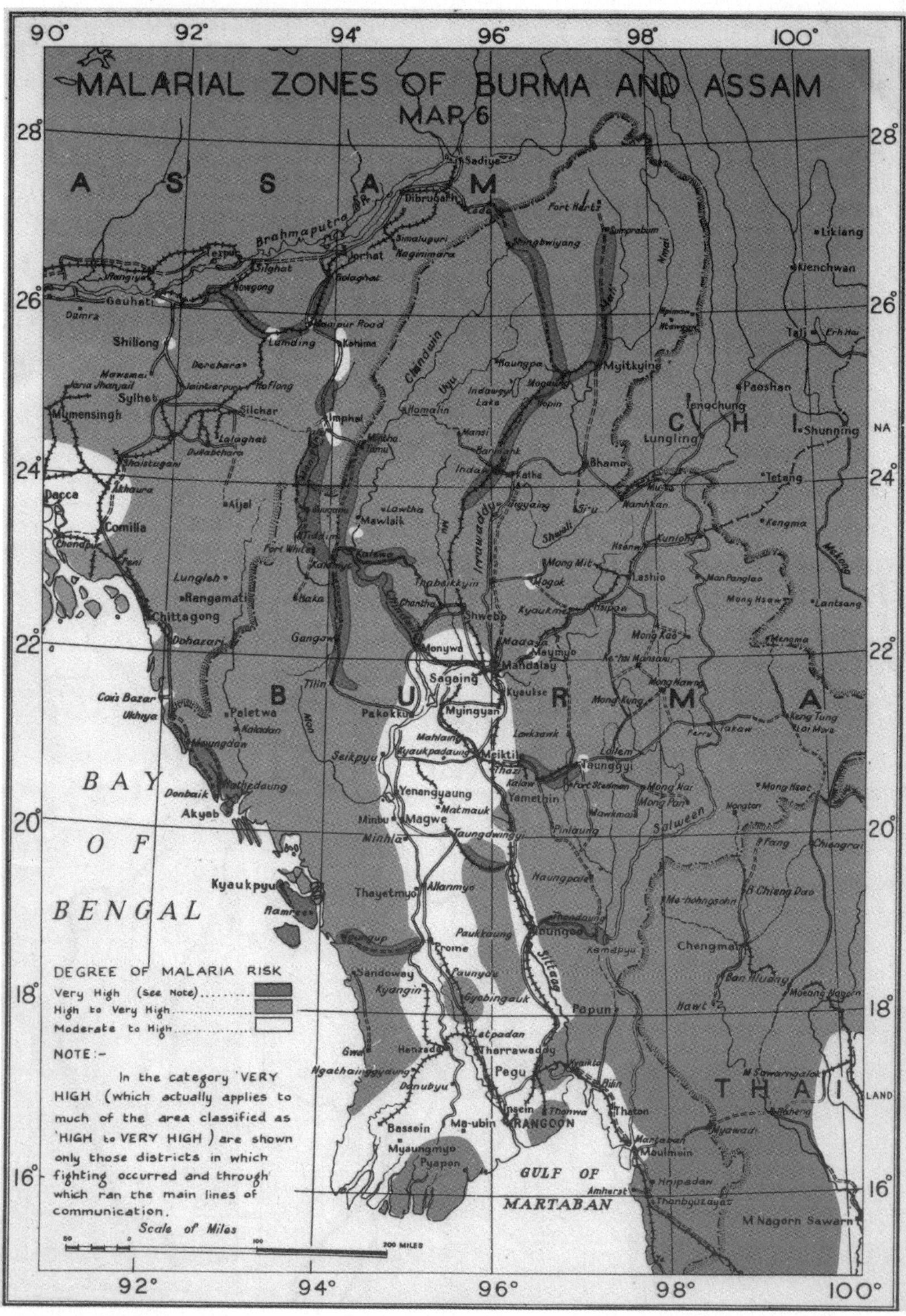

Mountbatten. *Report*, 1951.

Introduction

This is the story of one young man's war during the Burma campaign of the Second World War. The letters were written during the press of events and not from within the later national mythology of the War, as it has been termed. It is different from many of the stories from that 'forgotten army' in that my father, Harry Walker, was not one of the fighting soldiers. He was a doctor and worked in a mobile surgical unit which followed the front and he saw the injuries in that terrible campaign up close. But in writing to his honorary aunts, Annie and Flo, he says little about his unit's surgical work, and the sequence of letters does not in any way constitute a medical memoir. There are no instructive case histories and no details about technical improvisations.

Instead, the letters are full of the preoccupations that filled his mind in the intervals between surges of casualties: the delivery of mail, the quality of cigarettes, the weather, the food. The ordinariness of these concerns gives the letters an immediacy and poignancy that campaign histories lack. And, unlike many conventional wartime narratives, his questions and replies to his correspondents open a window on the everyday life of women. Back in Middlesbrough, Annie and Flo go to work, tend their garden, and navigate food and clothes rationing. Through the letters they engage in a back and forth conversation with Harry about the government's handling of the War, the end of Empire, and how the post-war world might evolve.

The letters rarely stray into deeply personal territory. He says nothing about his relationships within the small surgical unit and there is only a hint about the marriage proposal he made before going overseas to his student girlfriend, a nurse who also went on to serve overseas. But we can see his moods clearly from the tone of his letters: the boyish enthusiasm of his first weeks in India, his wistful longing for home and familiar places, angry enlightenment when he reflects on imperialism, tense and weary speculations about when the Japanese might be defeated, cynical rants about the War Cabinet's treatment of its troops in the Far East.

Sequences of letters like Harry's, once seen as of purely family interest, are recognised by historians as valuable primary documents. The military historian John Keegan wrote in 1976 in his influential *The Face of Battle* that contemporaneous letters and private diaries are 'much more reliable' than books written after the event by 'those whose reputations may gain or lose by the account they give' and urged historians to allow 'the combatants to speak for themselves'.[1] The lives of individuals can illuminate a period of history in the historiographical approach known as microhistory which focusses on a small unit such as an event, a year, a community, or an individual.[2] It has a relationship with prosopography, a method which examines groups of similar individuals, and which has also been used to study fields which lack good documentation.

But of course the letters *are* of great family interest, not only to Harry's family but also to all those families which contained a member who served in the Burma campaign and who said little about their experiences. Harry died young, when I was only ten. He was not a man who kept journals or letters and for years I had little to remember him by, mainly childhood memories and a few books and photographs. I knew he had been an anaesthetist in 'The War' but I had no details. Then one day my father's cousin Mary sent me a package of letters she had retrieved while clearing their house after Annie and Flo died. They brought Harry vividly to life. As I read them now I feel protective about his ups and downs, his naive grumbling and his innocent descriptions of scenery, as if he were my son instead of my father.

The letters are of their era, and some use words and phrases that would not be used today, but, in their record of a life out of time, isolated by distance, terrain and war, they are timeless. He describes the mundane everydayness of life, despite the surrounding battles, but most of us live lives in which nothing out of the way happens and, written as it was at the height of the coronavirus pandemic, this account of a man doing his best to remain normal in exceptional circumstances is just what the world needs.

Comfortable

My father's sister married a man whose surname was Comfort and she used to sign her letters 'Mrs Comfortable'. This was after the Second World War when she and her husband were living in Singapore, which had been liberated from Japanese occupation only recently. 'Mrs Comfortable' gives a sense of the still-colonial life of expatriates even in the very last years of Empire, so different in its warmth, colour and plenty from the grey, make-do-and-mend existence of the late 1940s and early 1950s among the bomb sites and ration cards of England. I can just remember the tail end of those years, the free orange juice for children, khaki everywhere in Army-surplus blankets and overcoats, and wonderful Christmas gifts from Auntie Marion in Singapore.

Harry's family was comfortable before the War. Not extravagantly so, but they were prosperous. They lived in Middlesbrough, in the heart of the industrial North-East, and were a lucky family in the pre-war years when Middlesbrough was one of the towns badly affected by the unemployment and poverty of the Great Depression. In the General Strike of 1926 when Harry was eight, almost half of Middlesbrough's working population were unemployed compared to a national average that was high enough at one in seven.

His parents, Edith and Harry Senior, were two of the pioneer white-collar workers of the late Edwardian era. She was a 'shorthand writer and typist', one of the first, and there is a faded photograph of her at her typewriter in a high-collared blouse and long, dark skirt. He became a dentist with a successful practice and their substantial house was in Linthorpe, the area where Middlesbrough's small middle class lived. Harry was their oldest child, born in 1918 as the First World War was ending. John, Marion and twins James and Robert followed.

My own family memories start with the Linthorpe house and with uncles Bob and Jim. Harry took over the family home after his father died, while Bob and Jim took over the dental practice. The house was wonderful for a child, with high, mirrored, mahogany mantelpieces, a 1950s kitchen and 1920s scullery, a playroom in the attics, fruit trees and vegetables in the garden, and an oil-smelling garage with a small door opening onto a cobbled back alley and to other children with whom for mysterious reasons we were not allowed to play. Uncles Bob and Jim were schoolchildren during the War and they became ebullient young uncles after it, erupting into the house or letting us play with the dental chairs when we visited the surgery. The smell of dental surgeries is my Proust's madeleine and brings a feeling of family and ease that ended with my father's early death in 1959.

Looking back now, my childhood seems similar to Harry's and I sometimes wonder if, after the experience of war in Burma, he subconsciously re-created a family life that resembled life with his father and mother, brothers and sister. He talked of emigrating to Canada, and many doctors did emigrate in the 1950s, but it was not a serious plan and he died in the town where he was born, in the hospital where he worked as an anaesthetist.

Annie and Flo

When they were growing up, Harry's parents lived in neighbouring terraced streets in Middlesbrough and their families went to the same Baptist church. Edith's father came from Wales, with its chapel tradition, and the extended Walker family included Baptist ministers. There were missionaries and chapel caretakers amongst its Lancashire weaver ancestors, with children who went to church schools and sang in church choirs.

Ann Jane and Florence Egerton's family were members of the same Baptist congregation as Harry's future parents and when the sisters were

Figure 1: Friends, about 1912. Harry Senior is on the right of the back row. Front row, from left: Annie Egerton, Edith Walker (Harry Senior's sister), and Edith Evans (who would marry Harry Senior in 1915). (*Author's collection*)

Figure 2: Flo Egerton with Harry's mother and the Walker children, Lealholm, about 1922. From left: Flo, Harry, John, baby Marion, and Edith. (*Author's collection*)

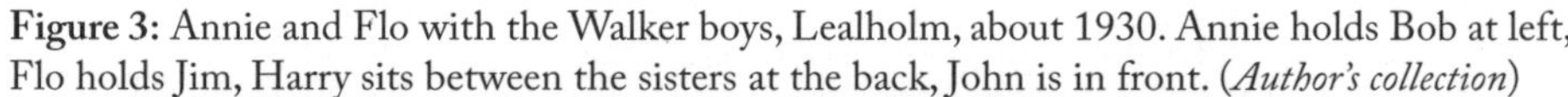

Figure 3: Annie and Flo with the Walker boys, Lealholm, about 1930. Annie holds Bob at left, Flo holds Jim, Harry sits between the sisters at the back, John is in front. (*Author's collection*)

Figure 4: Annie and Flo in the 1930s. There is a large photograph of the twins on the piano behind them. (*Author's collection*)

orphaned in their teens they were taken in by the Walkers. They were women of the generation who never married, whose sweethearts died in the trenches in the First World War. Annie became a teacher and Flo a secretary in the steelworks and they were Harry's honorary aunts, their house a place he could visit unannounced and where he could always find a welcome and intelligent talk. It is not surprising that he wrote regularly to them while he was serving overseas.

The sisters were automatic presences at family weddings and christenings. Annie, 'Nannin', was my godmother and their house was our temporary home after my father died. The 'Newham Avenue' he writes about in his letters is familiar, Flo's sweet-smelling *Daphne* bush by the front gate, the panes of stained glass in the front door, Annie's watercolours on the walls, its warm back kitchen, and the tiny bedroom over the hall, where I slept.

Figure 5: Annie and Flo with the twins during the war. Newham Avenue, Middlesbrough, about 1943. From left: Bob, Flo, Annie, and Jim. (*Author's collection*)

The 1930s

Harry went to the War from an inter-war childhood that was, in many ways, *Swallows and Amazons*. Values were simple and there was lots of outdoor play. His mother was a regular at the Baptist church, his father worked hard, his school motto was *aut disce aut discede*, either learn or leave. Middlesbrough High School for Boys was built by Alfred Waterhouse, the architect of such emblems of Victorian civic rectitude and respect for education as Manchester Town Hall, the Natural History Museum in London, and Balliol College, Oxford.

The old High School magazines are in the Teesside archives and turning their pages showed me something of Harry's schoolboy world. Outings and sports days roll across the pages, 'H Walker' mentioned occasionally as a swimmer and rugby player. There is news about old boys working as

Figure 6: Outing to Kettleness, Easter 1935. From left, John, Jack Blackburn (who Harry would later visit in India), Clive Richardson (another old school friend mentioned in the letters), and Harry. (*Author's collection*)

town planners and engineers and agricultural researchers in outposts of Empire. Under arch pseudonyms, the boys write pieces about militarism and democracy, or the deplorable state of house cricket.

Harry was a bright boy, the youngest in his group of sixth-form prefects, and he was only 16 when he passed his Higher School Certificate. He was also an all-rounder who enjoyed sports and the outdoors, and photographs show a teenager who took pains with his appearance, wore fashionable clothes and larked around with family and friends. His family had a cottage in the North York Moors and many of the photographs from his childhood were taken at the Lealholm cottage. He is a blond, tanned youth, grinning under tousled hair in the sunshine, surrounded by brothers, the school-friends whose names appear in the letters, and the 'belles', his sister and girl cousins. Every so often there were big family gatherings when the cousins and uncles and aunts assembled, travelling from Lancashire, Liverpool, Sunderland, Bournemouth, and even Canada and America.

Figure 7: Fooling around in the sun as a teenager, Lealholm. Left, polishing 'da flivver'. Right, with brother John and cousins Mary and Margaret. (*Author's collection*)

The groups of brothers and cousins and friends continued to fool around in the sunshine and drive to local beauty spots while the world took the first steps to war. In the same summer as Harry left school, 1935, the Ramblers Association was founded in England while Germany's Boy Scouts joined the Hitler Youth. The 1930s were his teenage years and, after he became a medical student, the Lealholm cottage remained Harry's holiday home, the images in photographs a little more racy as he grows up. He is polishing a car, 'da flivver', as he writes on the back in American hard-boiled film-speak; he holds a ukelele, a tennis racquet, or the first of the ubiquitous cigarettes; he wears a dashing white singlet and flannels, or tweed jacket and plus-fours when fishing or shooting.

Edinburgh

Harry's medical school in Edinburgh, run by the Scottish Medical Royal Colleges, was notably diverse. Its records show students from India, Canada, South Africa, Egypt, the West Indies, Ceylon, Mauritius and Australia, even looking only at the pages where his name appears. Some would become figures in world affairs, like Hastings Banda, who qualified the year before Harry and became the first President of independent Malawi.

The School did not have the religious (or racial) requirements of some universities and it had many Jewish students from America, as well as from

Figure 8: Medical students, September 1939. Harry and friends outside Surgeons' Hall, Edinburgh, at the outbreak of war. (*Author's collection*)

Figure 9: Students in the Physiology lecture theatre. (*Beck family collection. Reproduced with permission*)

Germany and Austria and other countries where antisemitic persecution was beginning. It is a little-known fact that at the time there were quotas for Jewish students in American medical schools. Even when I was a medical student there were quotas in some British medical schools for, not Jews, but women. I was one of only ten women in a year of a hundred

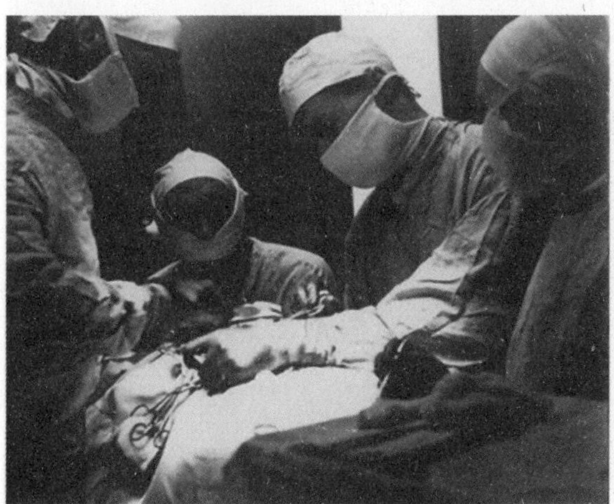

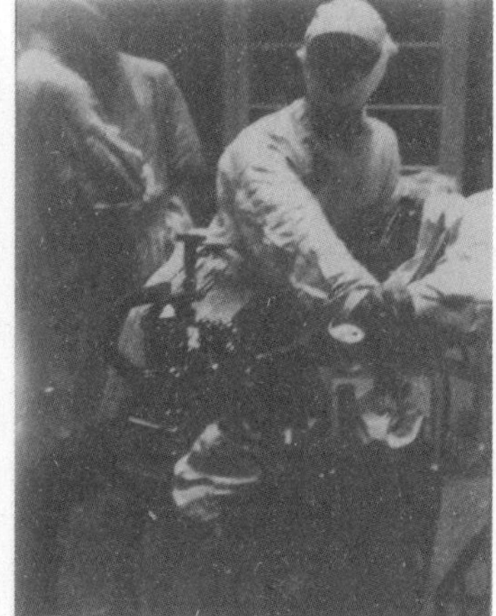

Figure 10: Two photographs of operations, Royal Infirmary, Edinburgh, 1940–1. Taken by Harry. (*Author's collection*)

Figure 11: Harry's friends in uniform, Redcar, Christmas 1939. Two names recur in the letters: Eddie Knott (front centre) and Leslie Murchie (front right). (*Author's collection*)

and Harry had rather more women peers than I did a generation later. Each era has its own prejudices, and that is emphasised on reading Harry's letters.

Harry became interested in anaesthesia as a student, which was unusual for the period, when anaesthetics was still to develop into the large and varied specialty it is today. His informal photographs from his clinical student days at the Royal Infirmary in Edinburgh have notes on the back about the type of operation and they give the names of both anaesthetist and surgeon.

It must have been obvious that war was coming, and that the outcome was uncertain. The Spanish Civil War began in Harry's first summer vacation from medical school in 1936 and some of the students went to Spain. Germany, Britain and France started to re-arm. The Berlin Olympics that summer is remembered now for Jesse Owens' gold medals, confounding Nazi racial stereotypes, but in fact international calls for a sporting boycott had failed and the displays of Nazi myth-making were a propaganda coup.

While Neville Chamberlain appeased Hitler in 1938, Harry visits Redcar with an old school friend. In Easter 1939, the pear tree is blossoming in the back garden in Middlesbrough and Harry leans nonchalantly against his car in Lealhom. He and his girl cousins visit Annie and Flo and they all take a picnic to Roseberry Topping and Captain Cook's monument in the Cleveland Hills and goggle at the 'very hush hush' experimental station on the North York Moors.

Britain declared war on Germany on 3 September 1939 and by Christmas Harry's school friends are in uniform and he is conspicuous on the Redcar Esplanade in his civilian raincoat and scarf. He has carefully listed his friends' names and units on the back of the print as if afraid the information could be lost to posterity: three in the Royal Artillery, one the Royal Army Ordnance Corps, and one the Green Howards. It was still the period of the 'Phoney War' when nothing much in the way of hostilities appeared to be happening and all these young men are smiling broadly underneath their military caps.

Joining up

During Harry's years as a clinical student, the war situation changed radically. The 'Phoney War' was followed by the German *blitzkrieg* into Belgium, Holland and France and the evacuation of hundreds of thousands of Allied soldiers from Dunkirk in 1940. British cities were heavily bombed and the Germans made advances in the desert war in North Africa. In December 1941 the Japanese entered the War on the Axis side with a stunning surprise attack on the US naval base at Pearl Harbor in Hawaii.

There was accelerated training for medical students and in early 1942, still a student, Harry came back home to bombed and blacked-out Middlesbrough to start his year as a house officer at the North Riding Infirmary. His interest in anaesthesia was strengthened by experience and he had given over 1,000 anaesthetics before he joined the Army.

(*f*) Any special knowledge or experience not included in (*a*) to (*e*)

Junior House Surgeon 1942
Senior House Surgeon 1943
(Some anaesthetic experience
– over 1000 given)

Figure 12: Harry as a house surgeon, 1942. His Army service record (right) notes 'some anaesthetic experience – over 1000 given'. (*Author's collection*)

Figure 13: Embarkation leave, 1943. (*Author's collection*)

While Harry was a houseman, the Japanese were easily victorious against complacent colonial governments in South-East Asia, defeating three European powers, Britain, France and The Netherlands, and invading the American colony of the Philippines. It looked for a while as if Japan and Germany might link up in northern India, but the Americans entered the War and there were Allied victories in Russia, North Africa and the Pacific.

As soon as he was fully registered in March 1943 Harry joined the Royal Army Medical Corps (RAMC) as a lieutenant, the standard rank for newly-qualified doctors. He went on an induction course at the RAMC Number 1 Depot at Church Crookham in Hampshire and then, in April, to Northern Ireland for further training in 190 Field Ambulance.[1] A

Figure 14: Margaret Wallace. Much-creased photographs which may have gone to war with Harry. (*Author's collection*)

'field ambulance' was a small mobile hospital. Harry later wrote to Annie and Flo that he 'used to curse the place when I was there'. He lived in a Nissen hut and the Irish weather fulfilled the cliché and rained all the time. There was square-bashing and the basics of weapons training because doctors, although non-combatants under the Geneva Convention, were expected to lead soldiers and to be capable of protecting their patients. The Imperial War Museum has photographs of their training: hours of stretcher-bearing practice and tent erection. Buttons and boots are polished, uniform is correct, surgical gowns are crisp and white. It is all very different from the few photographs of surgical teams at the front, the sweat-stained shirts, hurricane lamps, broken buildings, and sand, dust and mud.

The most important difference between civilian and military medical practice was a fundamental shift in notions of responsibility. The doctor's first responsibility is to his patient. 'You will make the care of your patient your first concern', as the current General Medical Council guidance has it.

But the Army doctor must at the same time respond to military objectives and timetables which require an effective fighting strength, and he must accept that he may be overruled by a non-medical superior on grounds of military efficiency. Like many civilian doctors who joined up, Harry disliked the Army's hierarchical, bureaucratic nature and his attitude is clear from his letters. But the rules, form-filling and standardisation were essential. In war surgery, any one doctor is only one in a chain of doctors treating a patient. Without simple rules and accurate records, mistakes happen and they may be fatal.

During his Army training, Harry kept in touch with Margaret Wallace, a Scottish nurse he met when he was a medical student. He brought her to meet his parents in September 1943 after he finished a course on tropical medicine in Liverpool. This was his embarkation leave before he went overseas in October. She refused his proposal at this time. The War precipitated some marriages, often with unfortunate results, but for other couples the uncertainty made commitment something to avoid. Theirs was to be a long-distance courtship, taking in his time in Burma and hers as a naval sister in Ceylon before they married after the War in 1946. There are two images of Margaret from this period which each have a rusty pin-hole from a drawing-pin, photographs which Harry may have taken abroad with him.

India

The voyage from Liverpool to Bombay was Harry's first trip abroad. This was the case for the great majority of civilians who joined the forces. 'Abroad' was exciting and strange to these young men 80 years ago in a way it is hard now to imagine. The novelist George Macdonald Fraser was 'dazzled' by the 'excitement and enchantment' of Calcutta. 'It was all new and exotic and dazzling to us, in those days before package travelling, when Britain was in the grip of war-time austerity.'[1] They had read about foreign countries, watched films, seen photographs, and many had an extended family scattered around Britain's dominions, but actually seeing, smelling, tasting, touching was another matter. Given this novelty, some of the descriptions in Harry's letters seem banal, but their very day-to-day-ness gives them an impact. This was his now. In his letters he seems less sophisticated than young men of 25 today, and maybe less mature. He was homesick for familiar faces and places, a new doctor with no idea if he would rise to the personal and professional challenges ahead.

India, including modern Pakistan and Bangladesh, was the most important part of the British Empire at the time, contributing two and a half million recruits to the armed services in the War, exporting textiles, iron and steel, and foodstuffs, building planes, and acting as a base for American action in China and for the British-led reconquest of Burma. The subcontinent had been increasingly influenced and administered by the East India Company since the early 1600s and came under direct rule after the Indian Rebellion of 1857. For centuries, Britons had travelled to India as soldiers, administrators, teachers, missionaries and businessmen, and its hills and plains were dotted with the garrison towns of the old Raj.

Harry's first letter to Annie and Flo is an expansive little essay written in best schoolboy tourist style on 5 December after reaching his first posting as a general duties medical officer in the 21st British General Hospital (21BGH), a military hospital in the ancient city of Jhansi in Uttar Pradesh.[2]

21st British General Hospital
India Command
5th Dec. 1943

Dear Annie and Flo,

A few lines to wish you both a very merry Xmas, and all the best in the New Year. I hope next year I shall be able to wish you the same in person, or if I still have to write you my best wishes, that it isn't from so far away.

I wish I were going to be at home for Xmas – I would certainly be coming round to Newham Avenue occasionally. Instead I shall have to think of you having your Xmas dinner, whilst I spend my time in most un-Xmas-like surroundings.

Instead of snow we have sand and dust. Instead of holly, palm trees. And instead of frost, a temperature of 70 to 80 in the shade. This is the Indian winter! Actually the climate is quite pleasant where I am at the moment. During the day it is just like an English summer's day, with a clear blue cloudless sky. It is a pleasant dry warmth, hardly enough to make me sweat. At night on the other hand it gets very chilly as soon as the sun goes down, and I change from shirt and shorts into battledress. And I'm glad to have plenty of blankets on my bed at night. I'm told that in the summer it gets <u>really</u> hot here – over 100^{0}. However, I don't think I'll be here as long as that. But I'll still be somewhere in India, I expect!

I had quite a pleasant voyage out, though I can't give you any details of the places we touched at, of course. The weather varied from a real Atlantic gale with bitterly cold winds and high seas, to absolutely frizzling heat, with the temperature, in what seemed to be a cool cabin, at 90^{0}! Lord knows what is was on deck!

He suggests that he won't stay long in this posting, which implies he may have picked up rumours about the Allied plans to launch an offensive to break the stalemate against the Japanese on the India-Burma border. But at this stage he expects to remain at a base hospital somewhere in India. Even quite late in the letters when the Japanese were retreating, he thought the Allied advance would take him into China, which was one of the options the commanders considered. He doesn't mention Burma. He also imagined he would be home for Christmas 1944, or soon after, and it takes a few months before his letters start expressing the familiar lament of soldiers in the 'forgotten army' that the Japanese would never surrender.

There is a hint of 'stiff upper lip' to most of Harry's letters, a sense that he is aware of wartime censorship on the one hand, and, on the other, concerned not to alarm readers at home. This reference to 'a pleasant voyage out' is a good example. His ship was the passenger liner *Strathmore*, part of a convoy that was attacked by German planes in the Mediterranean. Two troopships were torpedoed and sunk and six other ships damaged. He doesn't tell them about this for eight months and then writes that 'we underwent a dive-bombing and torpedo plane attack. I never told

Figure 15: SS *Strathmore*. She was converted to a troopship and was bombed in the Mediterranean. (*P&O Heritage Collection PH-04507-00-O. Reproduced with permission*)

you about that before did I? Something to tell you about when I come home.' Even when acknowledging this incident, he downplays it and looks on the bright side. It was 'an exciting business, but luckily our ship wasn't one of those that was sunk in the convoy.'

I spent a couple of days in Bombay and found it very interesting. There was tons of stuff to buy – both English and Indian, though prices were very steep. I tried to get a film for my camera – an ordinary 620 Kodak film – but even the Kodak depot had none and don't think they'll get any. So if you happen on to one, and don't want it yourself – it will find a welcome out here!

I went with my pals to the famous Taj hotel in Bombay – a most beautiful building much smarter than any hotel I've seen in England. Tea was quite cheap – less than 1 rupee each (1 rupee = 1/6) and the tea was the most delicious I've ever tasted. We went into the bar for a drink in the evening. Not liking spirits I wanted a beer, but apparently that also is unobtainable in India – even the homebrewed variety. So I had a gin and orange – price 3 rupees! After that we went T.T!!

Figure 16: The 'famous Taj hotel' in Bombay. Unknown photographer. (*Collection of Nick Messinger. Reproduced with permission*)

Arrival in India was a shock even to young doctors who had grown up through the Great Depression and seen wealth and poverty at first-hand as medical students. The Taj hotel is still a huge, luxurious seafront Edwardian confection of domes and Moorish windows, famous as the site of terrorist shootings in 2008. But long after the war Harry's wartime colleague, Paddy Donaldson, would remember that the 'foul-smelling odour of Bombay assailed our ship. Its origins were everywhere evident in the indescribable squalor of a teeming population in grinding poverty.'[3] Another young doctor contemporary, the mountaineer Charles Evans, wrote that he was 'suddenly plunged into India. My first impressions were of noise and squalor and restless movement, of human tragedy begging for relief that I could not give and from which I felt coldly insulated.' In the railway station he felt overcome by 'a crowd of beggars ... It went on and on and every kind of mutilation and deformity was offered for our inspection: stumps of arms and legs, blind eyes, festering sores covered with flies.'[4] The only way to process these contrasts was to distance themselves from local people and their distress. The military hospitals created this distance and were an Army-world of their own.

> I landed at my present address 3 days ago, after a two days journey on the train. I came with 2 other R.A.M.C. officers, and we shared a reserved first class compartment. Out here the trains are much bigger than at home, and the compartment was about 3 times the size of an English one, with folding beds for all, and a private washbasin and W.C. The native porters are funny. They just wear a sort of loin cloth and robe and turban, and they carry your things on their heads. They can carry enormous weights. Did you ever see my valise? If you didn't, you ask Mam how big it was. It took me all my time to even lift it off the ground, as it had in it all my camp bed, blankets, bath, coat, etc. etc. Well, one of these Indian porters – a most spindly shanked fellow generally, could carry it on his head with apparent ease.
>
> The hospital here is not quite what I expected, being half wooden huts and half tents. I live in a tent to myself - quite a nice one about 10ft by 12 ft by 7 ft high. I sleep, of course, on my camp bed, with a

mosquito net around me. I have no furniture except a folding chair bought in the local native bazaar for four chips (rupees). My clothes I keep in my suit cases propped up on bricks to prevent the white ants getting in and eating everything. We have no batmen as we had at home, but instead we employ Indian "bearers". Mine seems quite a good chap, although I can't really tell yet as I've only had him a couple of days. His name is the same as mine, only spelt differently – Hari, surname Chalup. He does everything for me except sweep the floor of the tent, which is a tarpaulin sheet, and is done by the sweeper – apparently a special caste of Indian; and my washing which is done by the dhobi. I take my meals in the mess with the other officers, but they aren't cooked by army cooks, as at home. There is a native contractor who supplies the cook and the waiters. Actually the food is very nice – a mixture of English and Indian foods. They are very fond of giving us bacon and eggs – with two eggs. And fruit such as oranges, limes and bananas, is very plentiful.

The chief trouble here I think will be boredom. I have one ward, with about 30 odd patients in it, to look after. But they are all medical cases, and I have little interest in medicine. Further they are all, or practically all, suffering from tropical diseases (chiefly malaria) and I know singularly little about tropical diseases. I suppose I shall just have to learn!

A Cushy Job Looking after the Chindits

Battle casualties were, indeed, light for 21BGH at this time but Harry's comments about tropical diseases illustrate an important point about the war in the Far East. Cases of sickness, such as malaria and dysentery, far outnumbered battle casualties. Lord Louis Mountbatten, the Supreme Allied Commander of South-East Asia Command (SEAC), wrote after the War that 'the terrain of the South-East Asia theatre was one of the most unhealthy in the world'.[1] As well as tropical diseases, leech bites caused jungle sores and the humidity encouraged the development of irritating fungal skin infections. These debilitating, preventable conditions seriously handicapped military planning and anti-malarial and hygiene measures were stepped up vigorously from then onwards, with commanding officers endorsing and enforcing medical advice.

General William, 'Uncle Bill', Slim, the commander of the 14th Army, spent considerable time training and re-equipping his Army after its disastrous retreat in 1942 and, although Harry claimed to be bored, the hospital was supporting military activity which would eventually lead to the recapture of Burma. An ambulance train arrived every few days, the number of beds rising from 500 to over 1,000.

This activity included reconnaissance and sabotage behind enemy lines. These Long Range Penetration operations in 1943 and 1944 by Special Force, the 'Chindits', were well-publicised by the War Office as a boost to morale. Immediately after the War several officers who led Chindit columns published books and this sustained the memory.[2] Chindit soldiers were brave but the effectiveness of their operations is today seen as doubtful. What is certain is that they suffered an exceptionally high rate of malaria and other sickness and returned to India emaciated and vitamin

Figure 17: Territory held by the Japanese in 1942. (*Reproduced with permission*)[3]

deficient, many requiring hospitalisation and no longer fit for active service. An American evaluation concluded that 'the technical resources and valor of Special Force were needlessly wasted by ignorance, indifference and intransigent prehistoric attitudes toward hygiene, sanitation and medical discipline'.[4] These attitudes came from the top. General Orde Wingate, the Chindits' charismatic commander, believed that much illness was due to hypochondria and wanted 'no passengers nor Geneva Convention people'.[5]

The hospital's War Diary throws light on some of the unglamorous ways in which attempts were made to bypass such command attitudes and care for the ordinary soldier. Soldiers were assessed when their officers viewed them as unfit and examined after their return from a tour of duty. The hospital advised on the supply of medical stores and demonstrated the use of mule panniers for medical equipment. Special Force doctors made repeated visits to 21BGH to discuss, amongst other matters, dental health and the supply of spectacles. A consultant ophthalmologist was deployed to the hospital 'to deal with the pressure of work from Special Force'. A section of the hospital was set aside for West African Chindits and a venereal diseases section of 100 beds opened temporarily with 'improvised latrine accommodation' to cope with 'a large increase in VD cases' in January 1944, a consequence of 'leave given to large numbers of Special Force'.

Meanwhile, Harry describes his 'cushy job' in general terms, respecting the requirements of military censorship. There were only about 25 doctors amongst the over 250 British and Indian hospital staff, so he may have learned some news from his colleagues, or even from his patients, about Slim's strategic plans or about ongoing covert operations but he was also very junior, too junior to be mentioned by name in the hospital War Diary except on joining and leaving.

The other nuisances are flies and ants. The flies aren't so bad as they might be, but they are bad enough. The ants just swarm everywhere, but they don't bite. Then there are the white ants which eat all your clothes if they get the chance. And there are some peculiar little birds which sit on a tree outside my tent and make an awful noise all day like a loud scraping noise. There are other birds with quite a pretty song, and some which chirrup just as Paddy the budgerigar used to. All day long there are dozens of kites (a bird like an eagle or a hawk) circling round and round overhead. Even at night time there is plenty of natural life – the jackals come quite near to the tents and howl and yelp all night long. And last night I chased a huge mouse as big as a rat round and round my tent by throwing things at it. It came in after

I had gone to bed, and woke me up by making chirruping noises like a bird! I had to use my torch to find it, as we have no electric light in the tents, only hurricane lamps. What a life!!

However it could be much worse. I suppose I am in one of India's fairly cushy jobs at the moment, much better than chaps on the jungle front keeping the Japs back. Still, I'd sooner be back in Ireland much as I used to curse the place when I was there. To live in a Nissen hut in a nice rainy climate would be luxury now. However, that will be something to look forward to for the next few years!

Meantime I must settle down and get used to a few years out here I suppose. I've certainly got plenty of time on my hands – work only takes up about 2 hours of my day. I've been reading Lawrence's "Seven Pillars of Wisdom" which I bought in Bombay.

I don't know how the mail is getting home – it may reach you too late for Xmas. But in any case will you show Mam and Dad this letter in case my mail to them has been held up? Thanks. Write back & give me any news you may have. All the best for Xmas & New Year.

Love,
Harry.
H. Walker

Some of the memoirs from the Burma campaign are infused with nostalgia for the Raj and consciousness of significant events in imperial history: Plassey and the East India Company, the Black Hole of Calcutta, the Mutiny and the siege of Cawnpore, the Delhi Durbar and Pax Brittanica. Harry's letters never reference history in this way and *Seven Pillars of Wisdom* is about as close as Harry gets to the romance of the colonial past. Instead a 'nice rainy climate would be a luxury' and calculations about the arrival of mail create a tenuous link with home.

Anaesthetics and the Arakan

Harry's interest in anaesthesia meant that he soon left the tropical diseases ward for a specialist battlefield anaesthetics training centre in a hospital in Bareilly, nearly 300 miles further north, and there is a six-week gap in the letters. Before taking up his subsequent posting to a mobile surgical unit, he returned to Jhansi, now promoted to captain. The hospital was preparing for a move and reducing its bed capacity so 'things have been very quiet'.

133 IBGH (BT)
India Command
2nd Feb. 1944

Dear Annie & Flo,

Many thanks for your parcel and for the card, which both came a few days ago. The soap was very acceptable, but I'm afraid the box of toilet powder had burst. The letter in the parcel mentions cigarettes from Mabel.[1] Thanks very much, but there was no sign of cigarettes, and the parcel didn't look tampered with – did you forget to put them in?!! I also got Flo's card a week or two ago – again, thank you.

I have ordered a food parcel for you – 1 lb tea, 1 lb sugar, 1 lb butter, 1 lb sweets. Not much I'm afraid, but the limit is 5 lbs, and the packing takes up 1 lb. You should get it in 2 or 3 months. Hope it comes in handy.

I can't give you much news on an A.G.[2] owing to lack of space, but I'll be writing a proper letter soon. No doubt you keep in touch with my doings by my letters home?[3] All for now, and thanks again for the cards and parcel. Lots of love, Harry

21st British General Hospital
India Command
18th March 1944

Dear Annie & Flo,

Thanks very much for the air letter cards you have sent me. I think I acknowledged one in the airgraph I sent you to let you know I had received the parcel. But I've had two more from you since then, one card from each of you.

Your garden sounds very nice, with your descriptions of all the flowers that are coming through. I wish I could see it, but I suppose I must wait a few years for that pleasure. It would be nice just to be able to drop in and see you for a chat and some supper as I have done so often before. Next time I drop round there'll be a terrific conversation, I'll bet! I expect we'll be discussing the peace by then, instead of the war.

Figure 18: The 'Bath belles' in 1943. From left, Margaret, Mary, and Marion. (*Author's collection*)

Apart from your parcel of soap, I haven't had a thing reach me from England in the way of parcels. So I'm still looking forward to smoking a good English cigarette. Thanks very much for getting the films, Ann. When they arrive and I use them, I shall send you any interesting snaps I take. So far I haven't been able to use my camera, as it is quite impossible to get film here, or for that matter anywhere else in India.

Did Mam tell you that I bought a parcel of foodstuffs when I was in Bareilly and sent it off to you? Or perhaps I mentioned it in my airgraph I wrote to you from there? Anyway it will be on its way to you now, so let's hope it doesn't go to feed the fish!

I hear from Marion[4] occasionally, and the other day I had a card from Mary,[5] so I am kept up to date with the doings of the "Bath belles"[6] as Flo calls them. The Americans still seem to be popular in that quarter – to my disgust! I don't know what our Kik[7] sees in them – lot of self-satisfied, smug, puffed up windbags. Why those lasses can't pal on with some decent English lads I don't know, instead of these foreigners! (You quote what I've said next time you write to Bath – I bet it makes them wild – Haha!!)

I wonder where Leslie[8] is going to, if he's had his draft leave? I'm glad to see he's now put up his second pip – you'll notice from the heading of this letter that I, too, have managed a little promotion. Someday they might pay me for my rank! But in matters like that the army out here moves "exceeding slow". I suppose it's the influence of India – time means very little in the East.

I haven't been able to get over to see Jack Blackburn[9] yet, as I have not had any leave. In any case it's getting a bit too hot to go there – he is in Bengal about hundred or 2 miles from Calcutta and by now it will be really hot there.

It's warming up here, and recently just topped 100 in the shade in the afternoons. But in another few weeks it will be getting hot in no mean fashion – 110 to 120 in the shade all day! Can you imagine it, as you sit in your sitting room, with a dirty damp Middlesbrough April day outside?!! The mosquitoes, too, are getting more numerous. They only come out at night, and we sleep under mosquito nets. I could do with a mosquito net during the day too, to keep the flies off. They are a nuisance, so damn persistent. Still I could be worse off if I were in the jungle so I mustn't grumble. I may get there soon enough.

'I may get there soon enough' suggests that Harry heard rumours that he could not disclose. While Harry was writing, the Chindit columns that his hospital had been supporting were moving into upper Burma to raid the Japanese lines of communication. Also, in these first few months of 1944, Slim was attempting to retake the Arakan region on the coast of Burma, to the derision of Japanese propaganda news-sheets which prophesied another British defeat. There, on 7 February, a field ambulance was over-run and Japanese soldiers butchered doctors, orderlies, and patients, a tragic incident which, indirectly, was to influence Harry's future.

For Slim, the Arakan operation would stop the Japanese from reaching Chittagong but was not the principal battlefield. He intended to defeat the Japanese in upper Burma. Since January, he had deployed troops to Assam and Manipur State and the vast, 600-square-mile, Imphal plain at 3,000ft, the only large area of relatively level ground between the Brahmaputra and central Burma, was transformed into a significant and substantial forward base. The plain was surrounded by jungle-covered mountains and dotted with airfields, airstrips, *basha* camps, hutted hospitals, dumps, depots and parks for armament, equipment and vehicles. Army engineers built 800 miles of drains, part of the malaria-prevention programme.

In February and March 1944, reports from ULTRA intelligence and from special forces behind enemy lines told of a huge Japanese build-up near Imphal. The Arakan operation was also secondary for the Japanese, concealing their Operation U-Go which, if successful, would cut the Allied air supply route from India to the Chinese. This would allow Japanese troops in China to be redeployed and would change the balance of forces in the Far East. It would also threaten India, and the 'March on Delhi' announced in Tokyo was not entirely propaganda.

But Harry has porridge for breakfast and an omelette with '2 eggs' and celebrates his return to the hospital with three friends in a Chinese restaurant in Jhansi.

I was interested to hear about Eddie Knott,[10] and wouldn't be at all surprised if I bumped into him ere long. I haven't seen him for 3 or 4 years.

I'm glad you got one of our eggs, Flo. This morning for breakfast I had porridge, followed by fried tomato, liver, and an omelette with 2 eggs in it. I get 2 eggs every morning, generally fried. Jealous??!! The food situation is quite good here, and has improved lately, since we got a new messing committee. The catering is done by an Indian contractor who needs keeping up to the mark, otherwise we get any old muck dished up. The cook is really very good when he feels like working and hasn't got himself drunk on rice wine from the bazaar. Still I'm looking forward to some home-cooked dishes for a change.

Do you see much of Mabel these days? Give her my best wishes, and tell her I'm sorry the cigarettes you mentioned as coming from her in your parcel seem to have gone astray.

I'm sorry I haven't much news for you in this letter, but things have been very quiet since I got back here. I haven't even enough work to occupy me fully. Three of us went down to the Chinese restaurant and had a really big meal to celebrate my return to the unit, but apart from that once I haven't been out of the camp since I got back. Leading a very quiet life, as you can see!

Closing down now, but I'll be writing again soon to keep you informed of my doings.

Looking forward to your next letter.

Love,

Harry.

Kohima

The hill village of Kohima was on the vertiginous mountain road between Imphal and the great railhead at Dimapur which connected the north-east with the rest of India. The Japanese attacked Kohima in early April 1944 in order to cut this road. Dimapur was 40 miles from Kohima and the Dimapur field hospitals were hurriedly evacuated, leaving behind only 66 Indian General Hospital (66IGH).[1]

The Japanese shelled Dimapur and despite their non-combatant status doctors were required to carry their service revolvers. Commanders withdrew female nurses to avoid a repeat of the rapes and murders perpetrated by the Japanese in Hong Kong at Christmas 1941 and then in Singapore and Java. Several hundred walking wounded were evacuated from Kohima to Dimapur in the second week of April before Kohima was completely encircled. But 66IGH had only two surgeons, 'quite inadequate' cover, in the understated words of the *Official History*.[2] Three further surgeons were rustled up hastily from elsewhere in north-east India and Harry was seconded there as an anaesthetist.

The fighting at Kohima was brutal. As the perimeter of the encirclement shrunk, the battlefield resembled the worst of the First World War trenches. Shellfire ripped the leaves off trees and there was a sea of mud and the stench of rotting corpses. The actual casualties were almost three times greater than had been estimated during planning: 6,500 sick and 4,000 battle casualties. The *Official History* states drily that 'the ratio of killed to wounded is unusually high' at 1:2.84. Wounded men lay on stretchers for up to two weeks in bunkers and were killed or re-wounded where they lay. Three of the fourteen doctors in the besieged village were killed and one wounded.

Figure 19: Kohima ridge after the battle. No. 9 Army Film and Photo Section, Army Film and Photographic Unit. (*IWM IND 3697. Reproduced with permission*)

On 18 April, the Allies forced the road to Kohima and evacuated over 300 casualties to Dimapur by armoured ambulance and by stretcher, 600 Indian soldiers acting as stretcher-bearers. Again, the letters show how Harry concealed the nature of war in his letters. The debilitated, wounded men evacuated to 66IGH from the siege had infected, maggot-ridden wounds, some with gas gangrene. Malnutrition and untreated malaria and dysentery weakened them further. But Harry is 'pretty busy' and writes about the weather, travelling and the scenery, as in a gap-year student's holiday postcards to his much-loved maiden aunts.

66 I.G.H. 15 A.B.P.O. India Command
11th May 1944

Dear Annie and Flo,

I really meant to write you a letter, but I am pretty busy, so am just sending an A.G. meantime. You will have heard from home that I am now "somewhere on the Burma front", and that I met Eddie Knott the other day.

The countryside here is very different from Jhansi. There it was all dry and burnt up with huge outcrops of rock, and little vegetation. Round here it is green, with huge trees and dense undergrowth and one or two tea gardens the only signs of agriculture. The monsoons haven't started yet, but we've had a few heavy showers as forerunners of the rain to come, and it's very hot and sticky most of the time.

Sorry for the short note, but I'll write a letter as soon as I have time. Write to me c/o Lloyds Bank Bombay.

Cheerio, Love, Harry

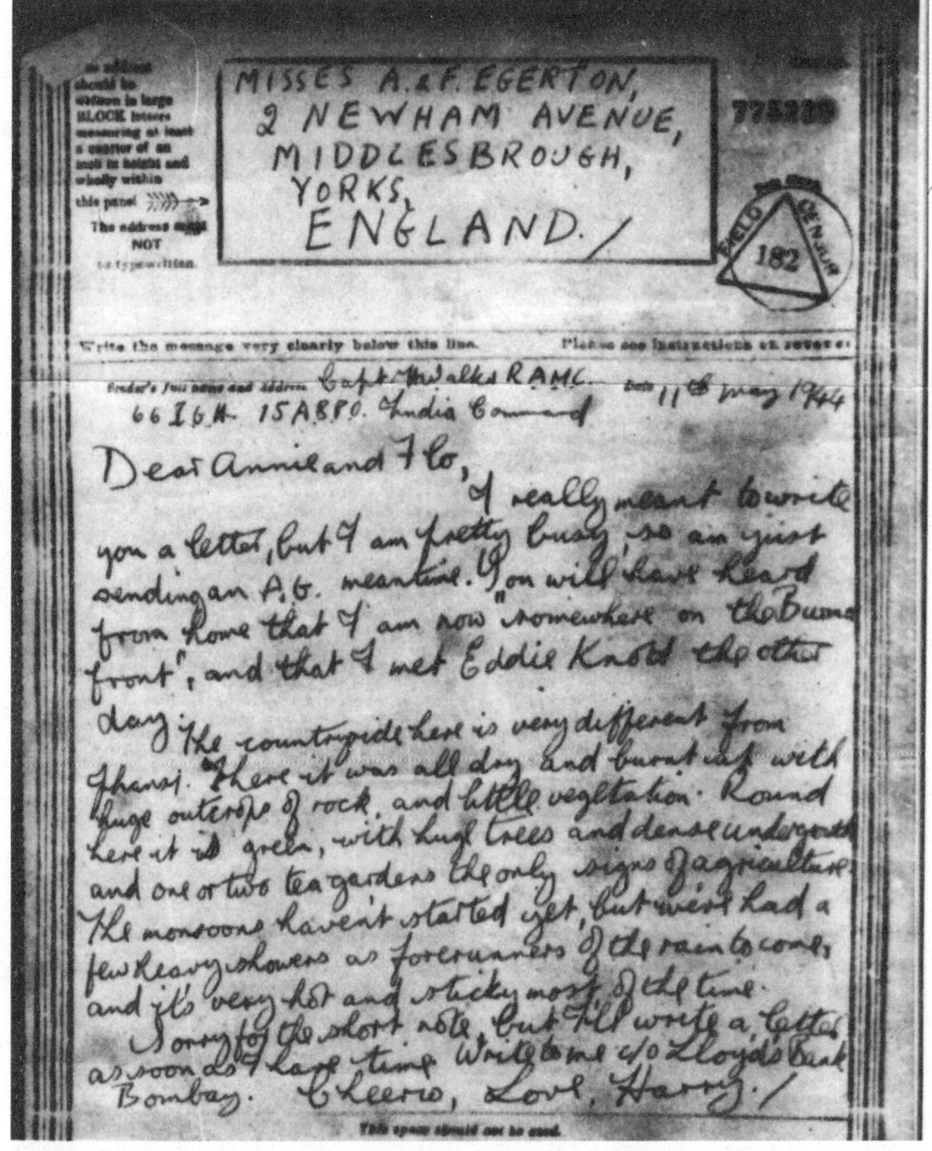

MISSES A.&F. EGERTON,
2 NEWHAM AVENUE,
MIDDLESBROUGH,
YORKS,
ENGLAND.

Write the message very clearly below this line. Please see instructions on reverse.

Sender's full name and address Capt. H. Walker RAMC. Date 11th May 1944
66 I.G.H. 15 A.B.P.O. India Command

Dear Annie and Flo,

I really meant to write you a letter, but I am pretty busy so am just sending an A.G. meantime. You will have heard from home that I am now "somewhere on the Burma front", and that I met Eddie Knott the other day.

The countryside here is very different from Jhansi. There it was all dry and burnt up with huge outcrops of rock and little vegetation. Round here it is green, with huge trees and dense undergrowth and one or two tea gardens the only signs of agriculture. The monsoons haven't started yet, but we've had a few heavy showers as forerunners of the rain to come, and it's very hot and sticky most of the time.

Sorry for the short note, but I'll write a letter as soon as I have time. Write to me c/o Lloyds Bank Bombay. Cheerio, Love, Harry.

This space should not be used.

Figure 20: Airgraph: 'I am pretty busy'. (*Author's collection*)

On 12 May, the day after Harry's airgraph, the Allies reoccupied part of Kohima ridge, but the Japanese held other positions including Kohima village on Naga Hill and they blocked the 86-mile road between Kohima and Imphal. They did not withdraw from Kohima village until 2 June and fierce fighting continued until 22 June, when the road to Imphal was finally opened. Naga porters acted as stretcher-bearers, often carrying wounded men 'across country that was quite impossible for British or Indian bearers'.

By Harry's second letter from 66IGH on 18 May, there is a pause in the influx of casualties, work has become manageable and Harry is 'very quiet' with leisure to tell Annie and Flo about his train journey from Jhansi to Dimapur. The 25-year-old Harry, never abroad before, is interested in village life outside the train window, the farm animals, Benares, the Ganges and the Brahmaputra, but Cawnpore, scene of a famous massacre in the Indian Mutiny, passes by without comment. He often writes like someone from a later generation, as if the Empire had nothing to do with him.

66 I.G.H.
15 A.B.P.O.
India Command
18th May, 1944

Dear Annie & Flo,

Here is the letter I promised you some days ago when I wrote the airgraph. I didn't expect to be able to write this quite so soon, but I've been very quiet the last few days as far as work is concerned, so I've been catching up with my correspondence.

This is a vastly different country from what I had grown used to in Jhansi. That is in United Provinces (if you have a map you can look it up) and was quite barren. The country was very flat, with hills up to 1000 or 1500 feet high rising sheer from a perfectly smooth plain. Here and there you would find a small native village, existing on one or two fields of corn, a few goats, and maybe one or two bullocks. The native cattle are very poor specimens, very thin and scraggy, almost always grey in colour, and having a funny hump over their shoulders. The natives also keep buffalo, wild looking beasts, black, with huge backward sweeping horns.

You seldom see any water – no rivers or streams or ponds, and the villagers water their fields from wells. The water is raised from them in huge leather buckets, raised over a primitive pulley wheel by two oxen, which do nothing all day long but walk up and down from the well raising the bucket. Or else there may be a primitive arrangement of cogwheels and an endless belt of earthenware buckets lifting water.

To travel over here I had to first of all go north to Cawnpore. Here the country is flatter still, but more fertile because there is water in abundance in the Ganges. What a mighty river! I changed at Cawnpore and then travelled east along the Ganges valley. We passed Benares, the famous holy city of India, but I didn't see it as it is a mile or two away from the railway. As you travel on, the country becomes much more green and productive; a change from the constant dried up, brownness of U.P. Finally though, as it gets greener the number of wells diminishes. Instead, the people get their water from "tanks". These are simply ponds, ranging in size from a few yards square to reservoirs hundreds of yards across. They serve the natives for washing water, drinking water, water for the fields, they bathe in them, wash their clothes in them and even use them as W.C.'s! You can see all the tank's uses being carried out at the same time on different parts of its banks. In Bengal, when the train reaches there, the vegetation is profuse, and there are tanks and villages almost every few yards along the railway line. Also in Bengal you pass India's heavy industrial area – coal mines, steelworks, etc. That is the part Blackie[3] lives in.

Finally I reached Calcutta – a most unimpressing city, quite the filthiest I have ever seen, with days old heaps of filth and garbage, yards long and high, stinking to high heaven, everywhere, main streets and side streets. The only thing that impressed me was the very fine new bridge over the Hooghly river, which from a distance, when you can

Figure 21: Howrah Bridge over the Hooghly, Calcutta, 'very like the Transporter'. (*Clyde Waddell collection, University of Pennsylvania. Creative Commons Public Domain*)

only see the top half, looks very like the Transporter.[4] After seeing Cal for a few hours I was extremely pleased to spend five days with Jack B.

I can't describe the rest of my journey here, as it would give away too much. But I crossed another of India's great rivers, the Brahmaputra – even bigger than the Ganges. In comparison I'll think the Tees is a trickle, when I see it again. And finally here I am, absolutely surrounded by dense jungle, still waiting to go even further into it. How I'd like to see the moors, or Linthorpe Rd for a change!! Write soon.

Love, Harry

The comment on Calcutta needs context. This 'unimpressing city' had experienced the devastating Bengal famine in the preceding year, with deaths in the millions, but wartime censorship may have limited the spread of information about it.

5th Indian Mobile Surgical Unit

For the rest of the War, Harry was in the 5th Indian Mobile Surgical Unit (5IMSU).[1] These were, essentially, mobile operating theatres which could move around the battlefield as required. They were usually deployed in pairs, alongside a field ambulance which nursed the patients and managed pay, rations, mail and other administrative affairs. Back home, Harry and his friends had trained by doing simulated operations, wearing snowy white gowns. In real war they worked under shellfire in monsoon rain, at the side of trucks, in tents, bunkers and abandoned buildings.

MSUs were deployed 'as far forward as practicable' to treat major injuries from mortar bombs, shell fragments, and machine-gun and rifle bullets. The aim was to stabilise the wounded soldier so he could be evacuated down the line to a base hospital. The first priorities were life-threatening abdominal, chest and head wounds, but the most frequent injuries they saw were open fractures and complicated limb injuries needing amputation. A soldier often had multiple wounds and the unit could at best deal with up to twelve to sixteen cases in 24 hours.

The emphasis was on standardised practice, and this was quite different from the autonomy that a civilian surgeon expected. The interval after wounding was almost always longer than in civilian life, and sometimes much longer because of enemy action, as at Kohima. Another major difference was the lack of continuity of care. If the state of the fighting permitted, the unit might retain a few patients to complete their treatment but usually the MSU was the first link in a chain back to a base hospital.

In almost all MSUs the surgeon was in command, with the anaesthetist as second-in-command. In Burma, the team often included a third doctor, preferably Indian and with a command of several languages.

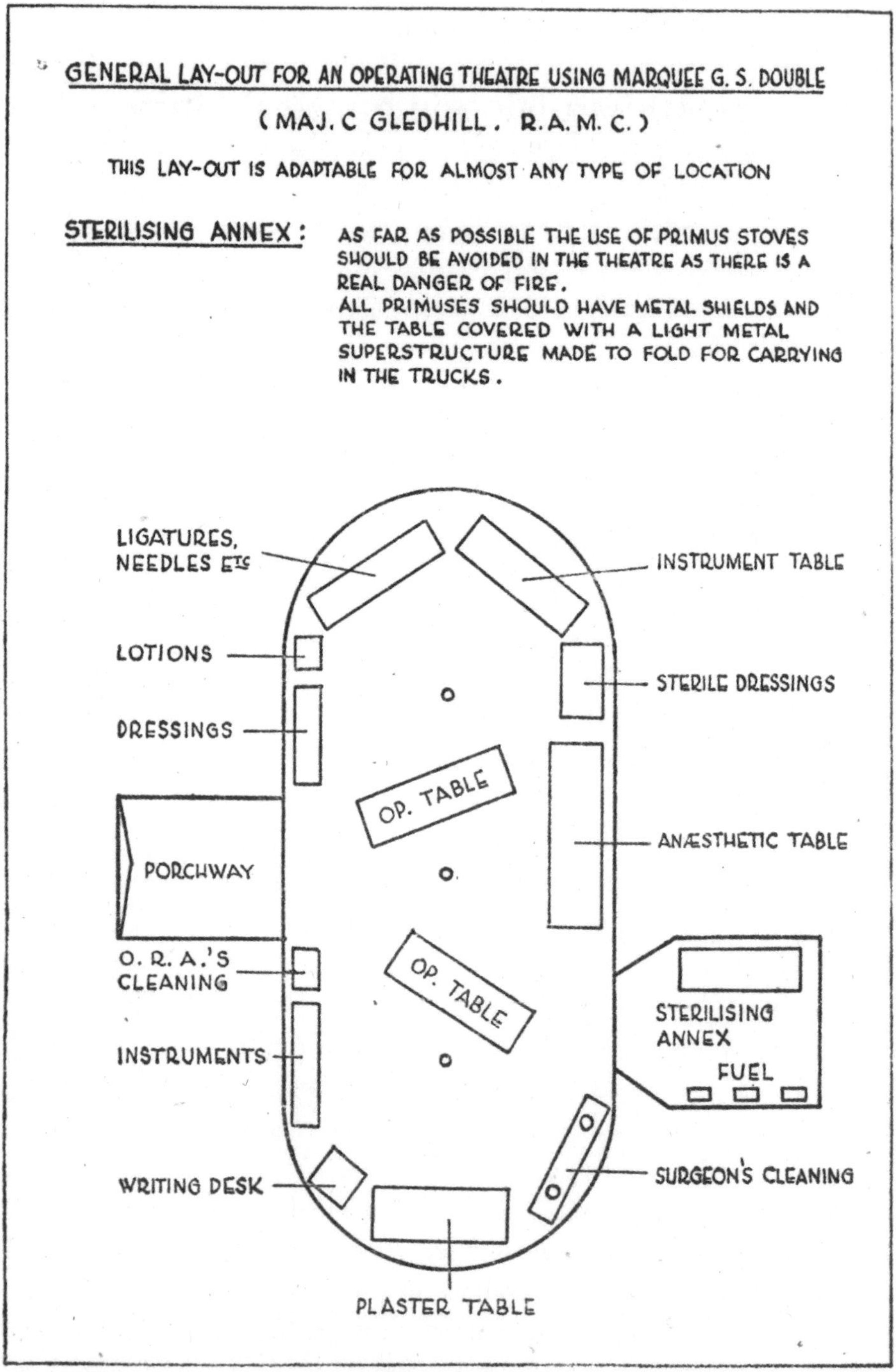
GENERAL LAY-OUT FOR AN OPERATING THEATRE USING MARQUEE G. S. DOUBLE
(MAJ. C GLEDHILL. R.A.M.C.)
THIS LAY-OUT IS ADAPTABLE FOR ALMOST ANY TYPE OF LOCATION
STERILISING ANNEX:
AS FAR AS POSSIBLE THE USE OF PRIMUS STOVES SHOULD BE AVOIDED IN THE THEATRE AS THERE IS A REAL DANGER OF FIRE.
ALL PRIMUSES SHOULD HAVE METAL SHIELDS AND THE TABLE COVERED WITH A LIGHT METAL SUPERSTRUCTURE MADE TO FOLD FOR CARRYING IN THE TRUCKS.
LIGATURES, NEEDLES ETC
INSTRUMENT TABLE
LOTIONS
STERILE DRESSINGS
DRESSINGS
OP. TABLE
ANÆSTHETIC TABLE
PORCHWAY
O.R.A.'S CLEANING
OP. TABLE
STERILISING ANNEX
FUEL
INSTRUMENTS
SURGEON'S CLEANING
WRITING DESK
PLASTER TABLE
Figure 22: Layout for an operating tent, War Office advice. *A Field Surgery Pocket Book*, 1944.[2]

Harry's letters rarely mention his colleagues but personal relationships were important in such small units and 'we were very much in each other's pockets', as surgeon John Baty wrote about 7IMSU in Arakan.[3] There were about ten or twelve 'other ranks', British and Indian. These included non-commissioned officers who assisted at operations and general duty orderlies who prepared patients, applied plaster, sterilised equipment, washed laundry and oversaw the generator and the supply of water. MSUs had their own trucks and carried enough equipment and supplies for around 100 operations.

Work came in bursts. There would be an avalanche of cases for several days, then time to catch up with record-keeping, and days when the unit would close down, pack up, replenish its equipment and stores, and drive to the next site to set up again. Later in the war, Paddy Donaldson worked alongside Harry's unit and wrote that 'during the brief periods when we *were* engaged in battle, the activity became frantic with the surgical team working flat out; wounded soldiers were treated first and then civilians [and then Japanese prisoners, he could have added]. At other times, casualties tended to be brought in at a manageable rate.'[4]

Harry's operation logs do not survive, but another anaesthetist, Robert Stout, gave his records, which cover three months in 1945 for 15IMSU, to the Wellcome archive.[5] The bar chart I drew of number of daily operations

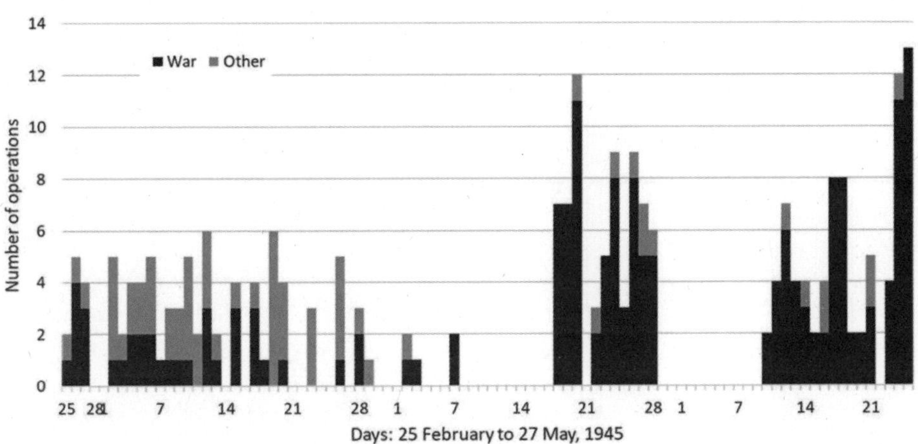

Figure 23: Daily operations, 15th Indian Mobile Surgical Unit, 25 February to 27 May 1945. (*Drawn from Wellcome Library GC/226/A5*)[5]

over the period of the 'race to Rangoon' clearly shows intervals with no surgery when the unit is in transit to another site. There are sections of the chart, Harry's 'quiet times', when there are few battle casualties to treat and there is enough slack in the system for the surgeons to carry out urgent everyday surgery, such as appendicectomies or hernia repairs. At other times, the number of cases is high and battle casualties predominate.

There is a buccaneering feel to descriptions of the work of MSUs. Groups of highly skilled, mainly young, men drive their trucks along jungle tracks, improvise technical solutions, 'liberate' equipment and attach themselves to Indian, rather than British, field ambulances because their food is better. It was 'a happy, confident brotherhood' and 'to see an advanced operating centre … at work during a battle … gives an unforgettable impression of teamwork at its best'.[6]

Imphal

The War Diary for 5IMSU stops in 1944, and the copy in the National Archives is a near-illegible carbon. But it does show that the unit was based in the Imphal area in January, before Harry arrived, part of the 20th Indian Division. In February it was near Tamu, just inside Burma, and when the Japanese attacked in March it withdrew to the defended 'Bull Box' at the all-weather airfield at Palel, south-east of Imphal. It was one of four MSUs at the battle of Imphal.

There was a shortage of doctors in the 14th Army and high turnover in 5IMSU in the first six months of 1944. The surgeon changed in February. The anaesthetist had transferred out in January and there are repeated comments in the War Diary of 'still no anaesthetist' until a poignant note on 29 February that the replacement is missing in action in Arakan. Harry was the replacement for the replacement. After Kohima

Figure 24: Palel airfield, Imphal. RAF ground crew load bombs onto a Hurricane. (*IWM CF 195. Reproduced with permission*)

WAR DIARY
OR
INTELLIGENCE SUMMARY.
(Erase heading not required.)

Army Form

...ctions regarding War Diaries and Intelligence ...ummaries are contained in F. S. Regs., Vol. I. Title pages will be prepared in manuscript.

Hour, Date, Place.	Summary of Events and Information.	Remarks and references to ap...

Figure 25: 5IMSU's near-illegible War Diary. Harry has initialled entries made by a colleague. (*National Archives: WO 177/2329*)

he was hospitalised with dysentery before joining 5IMSU and the War Diary records the delay in his arrival. There is a seven-week gap before Harry writes in July.

The Japanese attacked Imphal from several directions on 7 March and it was encircled until 22 June, though not isolated, because its airfields continued to function and it became routine to rely on aircraft for supply, transport and casualty evacuation. Slim withdrew outlying troops in order to draw in the Japanese and lengthen their already long supply lines. Non-combatants were evacuated, including some medical units, but not Harry's. 5IMSU was transferred to the 5th Indian Division. Slim had flown the whole of this division, with its equipment and armament, from the Arakan battle to reinforce Imphal. He diverted thirty aircraft from the supply drops to China to accomplish this unprecedented manoeuvre over a ten-day period.

There were six narrow roads and tracks though the wild and mountainous country round the Imphal plain and the Japanese cut them all. The Allies

Figure 26: Allied troops at Imphal. No. 9 Army Film and Photo Section, Army Film and Photographic Unit. (*IWM IND 3469. Reproduced with permission*)

Figure 27: Allied soldier with Japanese dead, Imphal. (© *British Pathé 1358.05: still 96. Reproduced with permission*)

were fighting from both within and outside the encircling enemy lines. Troop movements around Imphal were therefore complicated and the fighting was fierce. The Japanese alone are estimated to have had 55,000 casualties, including 13,500 dead. But Harry sums it up as 'there is no such thing as off duty!'

His letters become more reflective among the descriptions of scenery and jokey references to parcels from home. The D-Day landings on 6 June 1944 created general optimism that the end of the war in Europe might be in sight and focussed minds on when the Japanese might be defeated. 'I used to think we could finish them off by the end of this year, but I'm beginning to wonder if that wasn't just a bit <u>too</u> optimistic', Harry wrote. 'They are extremely good fighters, with very good morale in my opinion.... Nobody has ever under-estimated the German's fighting qualities, his morale, his equipment or his ingenuity ... I think he has all those qualities of the German, plus even greater fanaticism.'

5 Ind. Mob. Surg. Unit
S.E. Asia Command
5th July 1944

Dear Annie & Flo,

Yesterday I got 2 air cards from you (dated 16th and 31st of May). Thanks very much indeed – mail is extremely welcome out here in the wilds, where there is no such thing as recreation in off duty periods, and, really, where there is no such thing as off duty! I also received one from you some days ago, written 8th May, which I don't think I acknowledged, did I?

I'm glad the parcel of food I sent was in good condition when it reached you, and only wish I could have been with you to have a cup of tea made from it. That is a pleasure which will have to be delayed some time yet, I think. Maybe in another 4 years or so I'll be thinking "Well, I won't post <u>this</u> food parcel to Newham Avenue, but will take it with me and deliver it personally"! That will be a happy day for me, when I am in sight of coming home again. But it will be a long time yet.

They will have to finish off the European war first, before we can put in anything like an effective offensive out here. I wonder how long it will take to finish Germany? So far they have done quite well to gain control of Cherbourg and quite a long stretch of coastline. There's a long way to go before Germany's finished. I used to think we could finish them off by the end of this year, but I'm beginning to wonder if that wasn't just a bit too optimistic. If they could it would be marvellous wouldn't it? For then we might be able to start things going out here next year. But even then, I think Japan will take longer to conquer than Germany. They are extremely good fighters, with very good morale in my opinion. To view them as undersized, undernourished, ill-equipped, subhuman yellow beings who have no idea of fighting is an outlook which sometimes seems to be adopted officially, but which is in my opinion, a very dangerous view. Nobody has ever under-estimated the German's fighting qualities, his morale, his equipment or his ingenuity, and quite rightly so. No less should we underestimate our enemy out here. I think he has all those qualities of the German, plus even greater fanaticism. He doesn't in the least mind suffering or being killed – it is honourable and glorious to him to die in battle. Experience out here has shown that he will fight to the last man and the last cartridge, and will exist under seemingly impossible conditions.

Anyone who tells you the war is as good as over when Germany's finished is talking rot. We have to beat Japan after that, and that isn't going to be the minor, secondary campaign that many people at home think. The Jap won't surrender if he is surrounded, cut off and in a hopeless position, as would Germans or Italians – he will fight till the end even though he knows his position is hopeless. And that on a grand scale is what is going to happen with the whole of the Japanese forces. It will be no use our saying to them – "We've beaten your only ally, and now surround you with tremendously superior forces" – and expect them to sue for peace. They just won't do it. No, we'll have to beat and kill our way right into Japan. And that is going to take years.

I sometimes think we won't finish them off in another 5 years or more – it's such difficult and slow country to fight over here. No roads worth speaking of, terrible mountains, jungles and rivers.

You can only get a faint idea of what the country's like when you listen to the radio, or read the newspapers. Those places you mention in your letter – yes, I am not terribly far from them. When you wrote I was to the rear and the casualties I worked on were from there. Now I am well in advance of there – near where Eddie Knott used to be before the flap started. When he was here this was a nice quiet area – but now –!! You will have heard my descriptions of living and working in bunkers underground and how the Japs occasionally shell us. Sometimes we go to the foot of the hill on which our unit is sited, so we can see over to the hill on the other side of the valley. We can't see from here as the trees are too thick. But from the foot of the hill we get a good view up the valley and up the hills on the other side, and if we're lucky, as we were two days ago, we can see some action. Then we watched Hurriebombers dive bombing the Japs about a mile

Figure 28: Hurriebomber in action over Burmese mountains. (© *British Pathé 1366.01: still 93. Reproduced with permission*)

away from us. Other days we can see our shells bursting amongst their positions, and sometimes see through the glasses our chaps moving up into the attack. It's all quite exciting. But then the Jap gets annoyed and lobs over a few shells to remind us he's still alive and kicking, and if they drop too close we all dive underground into our bunkers!

I got a parcel of 300 Players a few days ago and since there was no sender's name on them I don't know whether to thank you or Mam & Dad, but thanks all the same! And thank you for the other parcels you say you have sent off. The one of mending materials will be very useful, and I'm looking forward to the book you have sent. Incidentally the times, given by Grigg[1] in the Commons, taken for parcels to come out here, are all tommyrot. He says parcels come here in 6 weeks or less. I haven't had one in less than 3 months, nor has anyone else I know. And I've just had newspapers which were sent in February and March – 4 months ago. His remarks about army postal services were about as sensible as any of his remarks on other subjects – all bunk!! He and Amery,[2] as secretaries for War and India respectively are a bright pair I must say! Not exactly calculated to inspire the British soldier in India!

I'll try to send you more food parcels when things settle down a bit here, and try to vary the contents. I hope by now your foot is better, Ann, you sound to have had a rotten time of it. And I hope Flo is over her flu' cold now the warmer weather is with you.

The address at the head of the letter is now my regular address, so you don't need to use Lloyds as an address any more. It takes about an extra fortnight for the mail to come from Lloyds, than if it is addressed direct to me. I got a big pile of mail yesterday, and it was all a month old or more.

You certainly seem to see plenty of Ginger[3] these days – I expect he knows where he can scrounge with good effect!

Must come to a close now but I'll be writing again soon.

Cheerio

Lots of love

Harry.

Figure 29: Jeeps on the Tiddim road. No. 9 Army Film and Photo Section, Army Film and Photographic Unit. (*IWM IND 4058. Reproduced with permission*)

The Japanese offensive in Imphal, the 'March on Delhi', was broken in early July 1944. They retreated into the hills and river valleys on the Burma border on either side of the roads, and strong bands of Japanese troops remained in the jungle behind Allied lines. Hard fighting continued. The monsoon turned tracks to mud, mist blanketed the hills, and these conditions limited supply by parachute and made pack mules essential, including for carrying surgical supplies and equipment. Slim's army gradually cleared the hills and the Japanese retreated behind the river Chindwin, one of the main tributaries of the Irrawaddy.

The medical units evacuated their treated battle casualties towards Imphal by jeep when the tracks permitted, and used light aircraft where it was possible to improvise airstrips, but they often needed stretcher-bearers and mules for sections of the route. Evacuation back down the line under these conditions was arduous for wounded men.

Figure 30: Mules carrying supplies. (*National Army Museum NAM 1982-06-58-25. Reproduced with permission*)

5 Ind. Mob. Surg. Unit
S.E. Asia Command
15th July 1944

Dear Annie & Flo,

Since I wrote my last letter to you a few days ago, I have had an air letter card from each of you – Flo's on 8.6.44, and Ann's on 16.6.44. Thanks very much.

The weather at home sounds terrible from your description – hot water bottles being used in June!! Nevertheless I would swap any weather you have for the weather here. We are in the middle of the monsoon and the rain is just terrible. At the moment of writing it is not raining, but the clouds are heavy and no doubt there will be a downpour soon. The atmosphere is constantly damp, and all our belongings – clothes, boots, cigarettes, writing paper, books, etc, etc, soon get covered with green mould if they aren't used for a couple of days.

We are living in a little wood, but the country hereabouts is mostly open, with no real jungle in the immediate vicinity. We are at the foot of the hills and look up a sheer mountainside, 2 or 3000 feet up. The other direction is a great flat plain, with a lake covering miles and miles in this rainy weather. Beyond that are more ranges of mountains, looking purple in the distance. Roads are few in number and very primitive. Some of them can only be traversed by Jeeps, and some only on foot or by mule. We have a lot of mules round our camp just now, and what a din they make! Some bray like donkeys, some neigh like horses, and others just make a vile noise that cannot be likened to anything! It's rather strange that these mules should be so noisy, for they are generally operated on to make them dumb – have their vocal cords destroyed or something. Otherwise their noise might give away a unit's position to the Japs. They are wonderful animals, though, and we would never be able to carry on the war out here without them – they carry supplies of food, water, and ammunition up and down the most awful hills, through streams, for hours on end.

The 5th Division was an Indian Army division and Harry was working with Indians and reading Nehru. He starts to reflect on imperialism and to compare political systems: 'You couldn't have a better example of a Fascist state than British India, nor a more perfect example of capitalism at its worst, with ourselves and the rich Indians grinding down the huge mass of Indian peasantry.' Many doctors were left-wing at the time and some were communists. They had seen as students the vast disparities between the healthcare provided for the poor by the state or by charities and the care the rich could buy.

It is good about Bob's exam., isn't it? I was very pleased to hear the result. I hope Jim does as well in his school certificate, and I think he should, after all the hard work he has put in. It would be nice if he could sit pre-reg.[4] in September and so start with Bob, but I think that's asking a bit too much of anyone's brain. Still, you never know.

No, Flo, I haven't grown a moustache yet! I may do, just to add a little interest to an otherwise monotonous daily round. I have spent the past few days reading "Glimpses of World History" by Pandit Jawaharlal Nehru. He, as you probably know, is a great Indian Congress leader and a friend of Gandhi's. He wrote most if not all of his book whilst in prison. I am finding it a most absorbing book giving a wholly different point of view from the usual English book written in very pro-British terms. If ever you can find it in the library get it out – I think you will enjoy it. It certainly has opened my eyes to the rights (few in number) and wrongs (many) of British rule in India. Nehru himself is still in jail, where he has spent most of the last 15 years – all without a trial! Such is British justice. My opinions on India and the Indians are rapidly changing, and are very different from my opinions of six months ago. I think after this war we should get right out of this country once and for all, and have done with all our self-righteous talk about our thinking of the welfare of India. Talk about fighting against Fascism!! You couldn't have a better example of a Fascist state than British India, nor a more perfect example of capitalism at its worst, with ourselves and the rich Indians grinding down the huge mass of

Indian peasantry. However, space does not permit a long discussion on these lines, pleasant though it would be. We can talk about it round the fire at Newham Avenue when I visit you again!

Though I don't expect to be home for at least another four years, even though the war with Germany may be over in one more year.

You will see me "on the road to Mandalay", and from there through China to Tokio, I expect. Thanks for the birthday parcel I hear you sent off – I hope it arrives safely.

All for now.

Love, Harry

Harry's reference to 'through China' reflects the prevailing American priority of supporting the Chinese, with a road-building programme and a huge airlift over the 'Hump', the mountains between India, Burma and China. But Slim was convinced that the 14th Army could defeat the Japanese in Burma, overland across the tributaries of the upper Irrawaddy and into central Burma, and he started planning for this offensive even before approval was granted by higher command.

5 Ind. Mob. Surg. Unit
S.E. Asia Command
July 31st 1944

Dear Annie & Flo,

Thanks very much for the parcel which came 3 days ago. The cigarettes and magazines made a good birthday present, and arrived at just about the right time – my birthday being tomorrow. I'm afraid I read the magazines and smoked the cigarettes without waiting for my birthday! When you see Mabel, thank her very much for the cigarettes as well, won't you? I also got a letter card from you Flo, two days ago. It had only taken 11 days to come out which is very good time indeed. And I think I have had one from you, Ann, since I last wrote, but I can't find it amongst my file of old letters. I seem to remember it saying your foot was now better, and something about it having been due to a thorn or a bristle or something. I'm glad you are fit again – you will be able to take better advantage of your summer holidays.

Though from your letter it doesn't seem to be a very good outlook for holidaymaking in Britain just now, with all the travel restrictions in force. Glad to hear you managed it, Flo – braving the perils of wartime rail travel, eh?! I would have liked to have seen "Arsenic & Old Lace" with you – I believe it is a very good show. You sound to be having a grand time getting your teeth filled!! Isn't it a delicious experience?! Don't you wish I were home so I could do it for you?? Ha ha – I bet you do – like fun!

We don't (needless to say) see any plays up here where I am at the moment. There is a mobile cinema floating around somewhere in the rear – supposed to be "for the boys fighting in the jungle". But needless to say (I'm repeating myself!) It doesn't get as far forward as this, and the people who enjoy it are the base wallahs.

Still, there are other attractions. The scenery is wonderful and we are sited on a slight elevation with no trees to obscure the view, so we can see perfectly all round. One side of us, about a mile or less away, are the mountain rising about 3000 feet sheer up from the plain where we are. In the opposite direction I can look about 10 to 20 miles over a dead flat plain to another range of mountains over in the east, and halfway across is a lake with quite a few islands dotted about it. It is a perfect picture, particularly in the evening when the setting sun throws the hills up in sharp relief.

The retreating Japanese fought hard, despite the monsoon. Their defeat was so profound that the Japanese left starving wounded men behind. The *Official History* remarks that 'most [prisoners] were moribund', confirmed by Harry in a rare communication of the reality he saw. Harry's jubilation about this turn in the war is clear. The news from Europe is good, the troops are optimistic, his descriptions of scenery are upbeat and his political opinions more pronounced.

And apart from the countryside there is usually something happening from the war point of view – though we are much quieter than we were up to a couple of weeks ago. Then, as I have told you before, we were a mile or two in front of our own artillery, who deafened us when they fired (which was very often!) And the Japs were very near – too damn near! But that's all changed now. Our chaps had inflicted enormous casualties on the Japs, and then to crown it all we put down one or two tremendous artillery barrages plus air bombings. That finished Johnny Jap! He pulled out in a great hurry, and we've been chasing him ever since. I've never heard or seen anything like our barrages. I suppose those in N. Africa, Italy and France are bigger, but here everything is concentrated into such a small area. When I say we chased the Japs I mean the infantry of course – not my unit! We moved forward a couple of miles or so, but the advance went on and on. Whereas before we were only a few hundred yards from the infantry, now they must be 20 odd miles in front of us – with the Jap still going! They're doing well, our lads. From their point of view it's a pity they are overshadowed by events in France, Italy and Russia – though it is very natural. But you can't imagine what fighting is like out here. Everything would be a struggle even if there were no Japs here! No roads worth talking of, swamps all round, tremendous hills, disease – malaria, dysentery, etc. One minute a burning sun, shining from vertically overhead, the next, torrential rain. Add to that a very tough, persistent, and crafty enemy, and you've got something.

I remarked in one of my letters home some time ago that I had never seen an ill nourished Jap prisoner. Lately I have though. The ones we are getting now are very miserable specimens – living skeletons, with wounds full of maggots. The retreating Japs have just left them behind to starve up in the hills. They are pitiful sights when we get them, and we've taken a lot recently. Also we captured a lot of tanks as you may have heard on the radio a couple of weeks ago. I saw most of them as they were captured only a mile or two from where I was. Some were smashed by our artillery, but some were in perfect order and I saw our tank men careering around in them. There was any amount of souvenir material, such as Jap helmets and nice shiny brass grenades which would make good ashtrays. But I didn't take any – I'll have plenty more opportunities for that!

I told you about Nehru's book "Outline of World History" didn't I!? I am now reading his autobiography – a most interesting book, particularly to anyone out in India. I must say my attitude to India and Indians has changed in the last few months from what it was when I first arrived. Reading Nehru, I feel ashamed, almost, to be British when I read of the things we have done and are doing here to the country and its people. We were so very pious and holy – holding up our hands in horror at the things the Nazis did. Yet all the time we had India in a perfect Fascist grip. People were thrown in jail in their thousands, without trial, for merely holding some political views the government disliked, and were kept there for years. In peacetime, Government here had far wider powers than it has at home in wartime under 33(b). Floggings, hangings, shootings, were all too common. It's my opinion that we must give India absolute and complete freedom as soon as the war is over. Otherwise I am fairly certain there will be another Mutiny – and I would be all in favour of the Indians. The more I see of British overseas policy the more I am disgusted – perfidious Albion – what an apt description that is!

Must close now.

Love, Harry.

Have just found your last letter, Ann (the one written on July 10th). Thanks for your birthday wishes, and the book from you and Mabel which you say is on the way. No, I don't think I'll be home for my next (27th) birthday! I somehow don't think I'll be home much before I'm 30 – but you never know. I don't know the exact date of my graduation, but I think it was July 1942.[5] If you want to find it accurately, ask Dad to find my Diploma – I think it's somewhere in the dressing table in my bedroom at home.

I was pleased to hear I may be getting some films from Detroit - thanks very much for asking for them for me.

Isn't the Russian army terrific?? Just heard the 9:30 p.m. (5 p.m. your time) B.B.C. News – they're less than 6 miles from Warsaw! We seem to be going slowly but surely in France, too.

Love,

Harry.

Burma Borderlands

During August and September 1944, the Allies continued their gruelling advance through the detritus of a fleeing, but tenacious and courageous, army. When Harry writes 'millions of flies everywhere' it means that there were hundreds of unburied Japanese corpses. It is not surprising that Harry was out of action again with another attack of dysentery. His unit was on the Imphal-Tiddim road, which went through an upland area where scrub typhus was endemic, an infection transmitted by mites that live in thick scrubland, a serious illness with a high fever. It can cause inflammation of the lungs, heart and brain, and one in ten cases died during the Burma campaign.

5. Ind. Mob. Surg. Unit
S.E. Asia Command
14th August 1944

Dear Annie & Flo,

I received your card (Annie's) of 25th July some days ago. It came in about a fortnight. Have I been giving the impression that your letters weren't arriving? I think they have all got here safely. You say you have been sending about one a fortnight. Well, I've been in this area 10 weeks now and I have had 6 from you Annie, and 2 from you, Flo. So that 6 means I have received more than one a fortnight.

Things are much the same here – still running after the Japs! I am quite fit again after another attack of dysentery I had a week ago. The weather has been vile – real monsoon rains, lasting for three or four days without a break and pouring down the whole time. Everything is mud! There are millions of flies everywhere, and the air is hot and sticky all the time.

Still, things look better. The news from France is excellent, the Russians are still doing their stuff, we are going ahead in Italy, and out here the Japs are at least definitely on the retreat. It looks as though the European war may finish this year (though I still think that's a bit optimistic and think it may last till spring). And certainly it seems as though the Japanese war may finish earlier than we originally thought it would.

That bottle of gin sounds very inviting, and I'm looking forward to a snifter or two to celebrate my return to the fold! Roll on the day!

You sound to be having a hectic time with the evacuees. I hope it's not long before we polish off the flying bomb bases, so they can all go home to London.

I was interested to hear of Leslie's trip, and Clive's embarkation leave. Les seemed to have a little excitement with the mine! It reminded me of my trip when we underwent a dive-bombing and torpedo plane attack. I never told you about that before did I? Something to tell you about when I come home – it was an exciting business, but luckily our ship wasn't one of those that was sunk in the convoy.

Sorry to hear of the demise of your apple tree, but the currant bushes sounds to be going strong.

Haven't had any mail for a few days, owing, no doubt, to the heavy rains and floods. Hope my parcels start arriving soon!

Must close now, but will be writing again soon.

Love,

Harry.

P. S. Your cable for my birthday has just arrived – 7 days to Bombay,7 more to here! Thanks very much for your good wishes.

Their independence gave these MSUs a flavour of dash and glamour but if Harry's unit was heroic, we do not see it from his letters. We see the quotidian, the waiting for letters that took weeks to arrive, the soldier's perpetual gripes about food, cigarettes and the government, the calculations about when the war might end. He starts to use the phrase 'forgotten army', coined that year by a Pathé News reporter. The

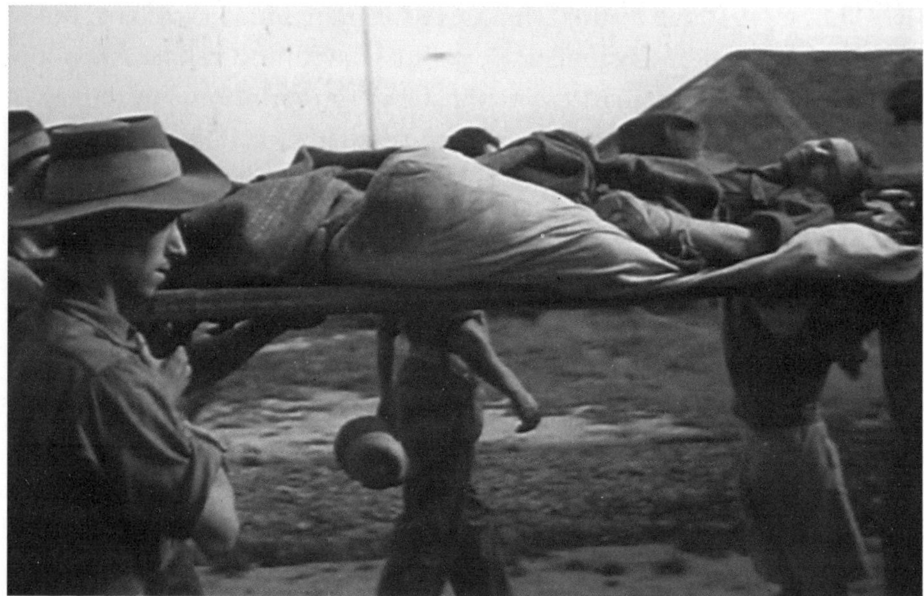

Figure 31: Allied casualty carried to an aircraft. (© *British Pathé 1948.14: still 48. Reproduced with permission*)

theme recurs in his later letters with the sense that their war was always overshadowed by the war in Europe. It is an accurate perception. The grand strategy was to defeat the Germans first and Slim's proposals for air assaults and amphibious landings were rejected and resources concentrated on Europe.

5. Ind. Mob. Surg. Unit
S.E. Asia Command
1st September 1944

Dear Annie & Flo,

Thanks for your letter cards of Aug. 4th & 6th (Annie) and Aug. 10th (Flo). They certainly were crammed full of news and chatter. It's grand to get letters like that – they put me back in touch with things at home.

I suppose things will have quietened down at home now after your tremendous influx of holidaymakers. It would seem to be an impossible job to travel anywhere by train or bus these days!

Very soon, I have no doubt, you will all be celebrating the defeat of Germany. The news from Europe is certainly terrific just now. Don't forget, though, the forgotten army of Burma, will you? I don't mean myself, but chaps who have been out here fighting the Japs for over two years continually in conditions worse than anyone at home can imagine, with minimal equipment and supplies. As soon as Europe is finished they should send home all the boys who have been out here for 3 years. Though if I know anything about our dimwitted friend G. he will find some excuse to keep them out here. G. and A.[1] – what complete b.f's. they are. Did you notice that A. told Parliament a week or two ago that we chaps out here were well off for comforts – because, he said, we can get beer more cheaply than at home! Actually, beer here costs Rs 1/2 (about 1/8) a bottle, very inferior beer, and limited

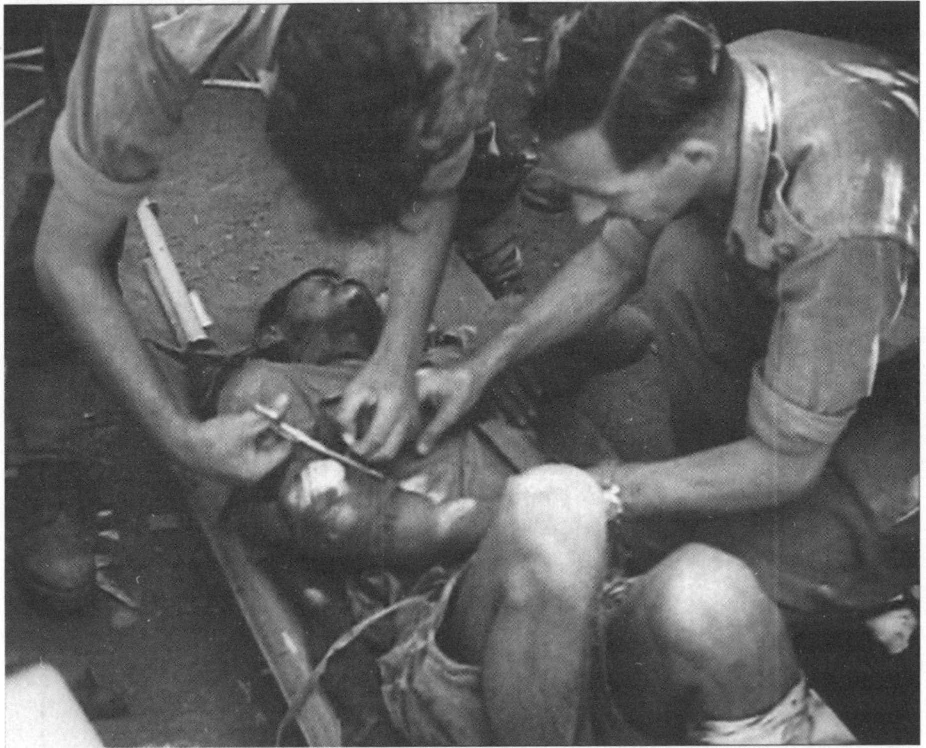

Figure 32: Treating a Japanese casualty. (© *British Pathé 1945.03: still 54. Reproduced with permission*)

to 1 bottle a week or less! I ask you, isn't he out of his mind? I wish he could be sent out here for six months, along with Mr G. – they would sing a different song.

We are in a pleasant part of Burma, all hills, a nice bathing place in the river, and not too much rain or sun. You would like it, I think, though the hills make Lealholm look like a plain, and the road to Danby Beacon is like a main highway compared to the stuff we drive on!

'It's grand to get letters like that – they put me back in touch with things at home.' These letters from home about difficult evacuees, wartime train travel, the garden with its apple tree and currant bushes, were a breath of fresh air in, literally, a stinking mess of mud. Harry's 'pleasant part of Burma, all hills, a nice bathing place in the river' is a camp by the Manipur river. There is a better view of the camp from Charles Evans, working next to Harry's unit in a Malaria Forward Treatment Unit. Charles swims near a burning ammunition dump and 'decomposing Japanese dead, unexploded grenades, discarded clips of ammunition and flies in abundance'. Above the camp 'it was honeycombed with bunkers in which were Japanese sandals, tin hats and water bottles and a litter of corn cobs gnawed down to the wood.'[2]

Yes, Flo, I think the idea of a Parliament at Newham Avenue a good one. Maybe I'll be able to take the chair in only a couple of years time instead of the 4 or 5 I originally thought, if we beat the Japs as quickly as we are beating the Germans. I'll have a few things to say! – and, I'm afraid I shall be more vehement than I was before I left home. How about "Down with Royalty" for an opening subject for debate? Followed by "No hereditary aristocracy", "No inheritance of money and property over a limit of £10,000 (say)", "Down with privately owned munition works", "Down with private ownership of coal mines", "Down with the Established Church of England", "That the British should quit India immediately after the war". Do you like that selection? That will keep us going for a while!

Either way, Flo, don't use an A.B.P.O. number in my address – just 5.I.M.S.U., S.E.A.C. Congratulations on your apple!! You will have a real orchard when I come home, I'll bet! Keep the gin safe for my return, and don't forget 2 or 3 bottles of good English beer!

I'm glad to hear Auntie Edith[3] is well again – let's hope she keeps her health. Must finish now.

Love, Harry

The Manipur river was in flood, the bridge destroyed by the Japanese. On 16 September a ferry was constructed to take the troops across. The medical units took their patients forward with them because the Imphal-Tiddim road back to the base hospitals was so bad at this point that casualties could not be evacuated.

5. Ind. Mob. Surg. Unit
S.E. Asia Command
21st September 1944

Dear Annie & Flo,

Herewith another report from the mountains of Burma. I meant to write some time ago, but didn't for some reason or another. Thanks for your card, Annie, which arrived today – only 11 days on the way.

Life will be much more pleasant for you with the partial lifting of the blackout. It shouldn't be very long before Germany's defeat will permit of unrestricted lighting. They seem to be defending Holland and Italy very strongly according to the latest B.B.C. News, but I expect our forces will break through soon.

Fighting out here continues to go well, as you will know from the news bulletins. Let's hope this time next year will see Johnny Jap nearly finished.

I chuckled at your story about the boys and the seasons. Shows what lines their minds run on doesn't it! I am intrigued by the fact that a lady wants to know what books I like! Who is this mysterious lady??! If I am going to have one sent to me, I should like "Riddle of the Sands" by Erskine Childers. I read it years ago and thought it a grand book, and would like a copy for myself, to read again. Incidentally, talking books, the one you said you sent off for my birthday still hasn't arrived. The parcel situation is really bad – I haven't had a cigarette parcel for ages, and I know John[4] alone has sent thousands of cigarettes. Some – x.x.o! In a cushy base post office job will be smoking them all. May his throat and lungs fester and rot!!

It's raining at the moment (as it does at most moments!). Real heavy monsoon rain which turns everything to mud. I'll be glad to see real concrete and tarmac roads again! But that won't be until we get leave, and there seems no chance of that yet. The whole unit wants leave, as we have all done about a year since our last. However, some day.

I wonder where Clive Richardson[5] will go to? I somehow had got the idea that he had gone over to France. But if he has been issued with sub-tropical kit I can't think where he's going. Certainly, out here the climate is hardly sub-tropical – it seems to vary between <u>most</u> tropical and temperate.

I'm enjoying life just now – no sickness, plenty of good food, no work – what more can one want?

Well, I'm nearly at the bottom now, so I will finish. Hope I get the book some time.

Cheerio,

Love, Harry

In October and November 1944, the 5th Division fought through mountains and highland valleys, dealing with snipers, mines and booby-traps, and taking hill villages. There were hundreds of Japanese corpses in the hills. They joined up with the 11th East African Division to take Kalemyo on the river Chindwin, inside Burma, on 13 November. The town with its nearby airstrip became the centre for several medical units. It is sometimes forgotten that the 14th Army was multi-racial and multi-lingual. Most of its soldiers were from India (including present-day Pakistan and Bangladesh) and there were Nepali Gurkhas, West and East Africans from many countries, and Burmese. The majority of officers were British but, overall, British soldiers were in a minority.

In mid-November, Harry is at 7,000ft, with wonderful views across the mountains and hoarfrost on the ground in the mornings. Although his letters do not reveal where he is, his unit was probably detached from the 5th Division to support the 17th Division's attacks on Kennedy Peak and Fort White in the Chin Hills. The brigade 'marched for three successive nights … and rested by day to avoid detection' and troops were issued with greatcoats and battle dress in order to keep warm.

5. Ind. Mob. Surg. Unit
S.E. Asia Command
17th November 1944

Dear Annie & Flo,

It is some time since I wrote, [I have] been hiking over these hills a lot, and [moved] camp once or twice. You'll get the details in my letters home. I have 3 letters from you Flo, and one from you, Annie, all sent since the back end of September.

You seem to have enjoyed your visit to Edin. Flo – I wish I could have been with you – I'm looking forward to visiting "Auld Reekie" again in another 3 years or so.

I'm sitting outside my tent writing this. I'm 7000 feet up in the mountains and there is a chill breeze blowing through the pines. Ordinarily we have a wonderful view from here over the Burmese plains, but this morning there is a solid cloud bank 1000 feet below us, stretching to the horizon like a vast field of snow. It is really a marvellous experience living all the time above the clouds, but it gets very cold at night, and everything is smothered in hoarfrost when we get up. Imagine that, in the tropics! It will however be warmer when we drop down to the plains again. That won't be long now, for as you may have heard, our troops have been advancing rapidly recently, capturing town after town and they are well across the plain below us. In contra-distinction to Europe where we are well stuck. As I said before – I don't think it will be over there before next summer.

Figure 33: Tank near Fort White. (*IWM HU 87183. Reproduced with permission*)

India's industry was hugely expanded to supply the deficit from Europe, hence the reference to the 'foul' Indian cigarettes and 'inferior' Indian beer. Harry's delight in the sublimity of the mountains co-exists with irritation and grumbles about his immediate surroundings. The everyday slog against the Japanese in difficult terrain, the harsh climate and tropical diseases, the lack of relief by leave or seeing familiar faces, grind Harry down and his bouncy early letters become tirades directed at politicians. Later on, 'base-wallahs' become his targets and, later still, Indians in general.

I seem to have roused your ire, Annie, with my reference to the "forgotten army"! I know we aren't forgotten by our individual friends, but I'm sure we are by the Govt. & country at large. And I'll give you my reasons, both general and personal.

Firstly, troops' comforts like cigarettes and beer. After 5 years of war, the Govt. has just decided to experiment with our cigarettes by putting in 75% American tobacco instead of rotten Indian muck as at the moment. The Yank troops here get real American cigs (Camels,

Figure 34: After Kennedy Peak. Buddha near Kalemyo. (© *British Pathé 1147.01: still 59. Reproduced with permission*)

Lucky Strike, Chesterfield, etc.) cheaper than we get these foul Indian ones. Govt. says we no longer get "V" cigarettes because the troops objected so. No now we get Indian Woodbines and De Reske, and some filth called Lions which even the Indian soldiers can't smoke. As to beer – we get 3 bottles per man per month perhaps – inferior Indian beer at over 1/6 per bottle. No English beer, though it is shipped out here despite what Grigg & Amery say – I saw it unloaded from the boat I came out on – crates of Worthington. The troops in France have beer flown to them in Spitfires – there was a photo of it in the paper a few days ago – yet we can't get any, and are not over endowed with aircraft out here even to fight – never mind fly beer to the troops. To send a lettercard from here costs 4 annas – troops in France send them free – I had one from Leslie. Troops in France get Ensa concerts and Naafi canteens – we get neither.[6] They have decided to give Japanese campaign pay, in view of the awful conditions here, yet won't backdate it for troops who've been against the Japs for 2 years & more – why? And at the same time as they give me £1 a week Jap pay they take off my Field Allowance of 45 rupees a month (= over £3 monthly) so I'm no better off. What a benevolent government we have – the b----s! The crowning thing for me is that I have just had Rs 240 odd docked off my pay for lodging over the past 6 months! Considering that the most luxurious accommodation has been a tent 6ft by 4ft which wouldn't have cost Rs 240, and that for at least one month I lived in a hole dug in the ground, being shelled every day, I think the Govt. has some nerve to charge me the equivalent of almost £1 a week for lodgings!

Don't say we're not forgotten – the Govt. knows we're here but prefers to ignore us, or if it remembers us, it is only to apply pinpricks. Damn the whole pack of them from Churchill down! A more hypocritical bunch of slimy Imperialists couldn't be. Fighting for democracy – nuts! Fighting for vested interests, capitalism, inequality, and Britain's own brand of Fascism – Imperialism.

Well, think that lot out!! I've just sent off your Xmas card – hope it arrives in time. Love,

Harry

He was not the only doctor to grumble about conditions. John Baty also complained about pay deductions for 'heat and light' and wrote reports to New Delhi making suggestions about improvements in equipment. Despite his contempt for politicians, Harry is at least quick to correct some of his rants when he learns that his assumptions were mistaken.

5. Ind. Mob. Surg. Unit
S.E. Asia Command
29th November 1944

Dear Annie & Flo,

I just received another card from you, Ann, dated Nov. 11th.

You seem to have a hectic time with your shopping these days – I refer to your story about your new hat!

The house sounds very smart in its new coat of paint. I'll be afraid to enter such a posh establishment when I get home after living for years in tents in the jungle!

No, I haven't received any Xmas parcels yet – but I'm looking forward to seeing one or two! Your parcel sounds as though it will take a day or 2 to open – though that is all to the good – you'd be amazed to see the battered condition parcels reach here in. Talking about parcels – didn't you send me films for my camera – ages ago? I haven't received them yet, and it must be 7 or 8 months since you told me you were sending them. I wish I could get some, as I only have one film left – one of the two Auntie Edith and Uncle Matt[7] sent – the only two I have ever received. They are unobtainable out here – at least my size – 620 – are not available. I am also looking forward to the magazines and books you mention. Did you ever get my letter saying I would like "Riddle of the Sands" by Erskine Childers? In answer to the mysterious lady who wanted to buy me a book?

By the way, I made a mistake in my last letter. Remember I complained that I had been charged lodging for the past few months – Rs 240 odd? Well I was wrong I find on investigation. I shall explain. In India a captain R.A.M.C. gets Rs 45 a month lodging allowance, and if he gets lodgings provided, all or some of that amount is deducted to pay for it. Apparently once I enter a combat area this lodging allowance is stopped – yet no lodgings are provided. So I get no quarters and no money in lieu. And the 240 rupees was a deduction of a few months lodging allowance they had paid me by mistake since I entered this area. So, don't let the Government mislead you into thinking they are generous by giving me £1 a week Jap campaign pay (about 13 rupees a week – about 50 odd rupees a month). Actually I am worse off financially by fighting the Japs as they have docked my 45 rupees a month lodging allowance and 30 rupees a month field allowance since I entered the Jap campaign area. I'd be better off as far as money goes if I were nowhere near the Japs. Good old British government – they are <u>so</u> benevolent to the men they sent to war, aren't they??

We've been living in luxury recently on American beer and cigarettes bought from some Yank ambulance drivers.[8] Just exactly the same as they buy at home in U.S.A. They get (each man) a crate of beer, 800 cigarettes, chocolate, sweets, tins of fruit & fruit & tomato juice, soap, shaving cream, writing paper, etc. They pay for it at very cheap rates. And what do we get from our Govt. – firstly excuses that there is no shipping space, and then when that is exposed as bunk, the excuse that English stuff won't keep in the tropics – absolute piffle for American stuff keeps, and English stuff did in peacetime when they exported it. However we are resigned to getting nothing out of Churchill and Co except so much hot air, so why worry?

I was sorry to hear Eddie Knott was ill – that explains why he hasn't answered my letter to him. Lucky man to get home in another 2 or 3 months. His sprue should settle once he gets into a temperate climate – it's a sort of chronic dysentery or colitis, with anaemia.

Must close now,
Love,
Harry.

At the end of 1944 the 5th Division moved back to Imphal for rest and refitting, but Harry's unit remained at the front. This circumstance may have added piquancy to his opinions about life in the Army. But his mood is lifting with the prospect of Christmas and a 'good do – just a marquee with food & drink on tables' and 'a glass of beer now & then'. He is starting to laugh at himself and his 'grouses'.

5. Ind. Mob. Surg. Unit
S. E. Asia Command
23rd December 1944

Dear Annie & Flo,

I've had a lot of mail from you over the past week or so. Your parcels arrived safely, complete with toilet articles, papers & mags, cigarettes, biscuits, films (thanks <u>very</u> much for them) and enough tablets & pastilles to cure all my colds and tummyaches till the [end] of the war! Thanks very much indeed for all you have sent me, and please thank Mabel for her share.

I've also had a few letter cards from you – three from you Flo – 30th August (that took a long time!), 22nd Nov. and 8th Dec. And 2 from you Ann – 3rd and 5th Dec, also a greetings A.G.

Well, as I write, we are just getting ready for Xmas. The unit to which we are attached are throwing a party tomorrow night (Xmas Eve) and expect about 70 officers from nearby units. Should be a good do – just a marquee with food & drink on tables – help yourself, no service – and may the best man win!

Today I've been collecting our unit's booze ration – 1 whisky, 2 gin, 3 beer per officer, and 3 beer per man. I can't say I'm struck on the hard tack, but I like a glass of beer now & then. However, I'll sell off my spirits to whoever wants it, and keep the other half to offer any friends who come over Xmas & New Year.

Talking of booze, did you see Churchill's announcement on conditions in S.E.A.C? Sounds as though things will be improved some day. Maybe it will get so good I'll have nothing to grouse at!! (Unlikely, I think!) Though I must take back one of my more recent grouses – i.e. that although we now get Jap campaign pay, we lose our field allowance. Apparently I was misinformed on that point, for we still get field allowance! However, that still doesn't make me any fonder of the powers that be – I am chronically "agin the government"!

What a surprise about Margaret![9] I must write to congratulate her. Her fiancé (or rather, husband, now) is a lucky lad to get home leave. But, for myself I would sooner stay here and wait for my repatriation in another 2½ years. I couldn't stand having a month at home, looking forward to returning to the jungle – I'd go barmy!

We are quiet here for the moment, collecting new stores ready to go into action soon. We haven't been so far from the fighting for months – I hope they don't take Mandalay before I get a chance to see it!

This seems to be the only successful front at the moment (with the Philippines). The Germans certainly pulled a fast one in Europe. That will shake up a few dolts at home who had slackened off, thinking it was as good as over! I see they are calling up another 1/2 million at home – the Govt. must be expecting a long war yet. Ah me!

Closing down now.

Love,

Harry.

Irrawaddy Shore

Slim's immediate goal now for the main force was to cross the Chindwin and move to the Irrawaddy. He planned lesser advances in Arakan to capture airfields, and in north-east Burma by the Chinese. He would gain access to the Irrawaddy's transport links throughout Burma and the country's main railway would be within reach, together with strategic airfields and the cities of Meiktila and Mandalay. The terrain was open plains so that tanks and mobile artillery could be deployed.

In December 1944 and January 1945 the 14th Army captured significant sites in central Burma. To get there, army engineers had made roads, thrown Bailey bridges across rivers and felled forests to build river barges. When Harry wrote his next letters in February, the Irrawaddy crossing was imminent. His unit was back in the British 2nd Division and he sounds serene under his pagoda on the Shwebo plain, 'a lovely tall snow white temple. Its top is festooned with little brass bells which tinkle pleasantly in the breeze.'

5. Ind. Mob. Surg. Unit
S.E. Asia Command
2nd February 1945

Dear Annie & Flo,

Sorry I haven't written for so long a time, but until 2 days ago I hadn't heard from you for quite some time, and I was waiting for something from you to reply to. Day before yesterday I got your A.G. Ann, dated 29.12.44 and numbered 2. I haven't, so date, received number 1!

You will have had, by now, my letter thanking you for your Xmas parcel, containing the films. Yes, I think the films from your cousin

Figure 35: Pagodas near Shwebo, January 1945. Taken by Harry. (*Author's collection*)

in America must have gone the same way as many of my cigarettes. Did I ever write and tell you about the mistake I made with your Xmas parcel you sent me? I wrote to Mam & Dad telling them how I had received it, and expressing amazement at the amount of cough lozenges, stomach powders, etc. you put in! It was only after I had written that that I opened the various tins and discovered that except for one tin of cough lozenges, they all contained cigarettes! I did laugh at my mistake, but needless to say I was glad, when I saw the cigs, that it had been a mistake!

Life is very pleasant with me just now. It gets a bit noisy occasionally with the guns going off nearby, and bombers plastering the Japs a mile or two away. But that, as I say, that is only occasional and doesn't bother us – though it's certain the Jap has quite a headache!

Our camp is built around a pagoda – a lovely tall snow white temple. Its top is festooned with little brass bells which tinkle pleasantly in the breeze. Just now the weather is beginning to warm up – has done so quite suddenly in the past few days – and in the afternoons and evenings it is quite sticky with the thermometer at 95°. It will get much hotter by March and April – 110° or more. Still, by then we'll be acclimatised to heat again. At the moment I feel it somewhat, after a few months in the hills with a climate like home, or colder.

I bet my talking of heat in February sounds strange to you, doesn't it? On the B.B.C. last night they were talking of the severe weather at home last month – how the E. Riding was cut off by snow drifts, and how trains from Scotland were arriving in London hours late and covered in icicles! I don't expect to see any snow or ice until I reach home again – unless they have freak weather when we get to Malaya, Siam, Indo China or wherever we go after Burma!

I am intrigued at your mention of Kirby School[1] and our visits there at the beginning of the war. I presume you are referring to the nights spent in the air raid shelters there? Don't tell me you're having the same racket again? What is it this time – bombers or V2 rockets?

I got a copy of Margaret's wedding photo – it's very nice, isn't it? I hear Uncle Matt is in bed ill – I hope he is better soon.

I'm looking forward to reading the magazines and 'Riddle of the Sands'. I don't seem to have had any reading matter for some time now.

Well, I'll close now. For once I haven't entered upon my customary political tirade – but don't worry – I'll treat you to another one soon! Up the Reds – out with Churchill and his gutless, witless crew of stooges! Down with royalty. Free beer and bus rides for all! Hooray!!

Love, Harry.

At this point, the division was preparing to cross the vast Irrawaddy against a defence by the Japanese on the opposite bank. The troops were amongst a civilian population where 'smallpox was common and plague not unknown'.

5. Ind. Mob. Surg. Unit
S.E. Asia Command
10th February 1945

Dear Annie & Flo,

I had just posted my last letter to you, when your letter arrived, Flo. And 2 days ago I got one from you, Ann. So I must bring my correspondence up to date and write to you again! Isn't it strange how erratic the mails are? Flo's letter written a day after Annie's arrived about 3 or 4 days before it! But I can't grumble about my mail recently, – I've had a few letters which took only 8 days to arrive from England. And now they have decided to allow us to send all our air mail stuff free of charge, and also cut the price from home to only 1½d – a great concession. Government have acted quickly and effectively on Munster's[2] recommendation about postal services. It will be very pleasing if they take similar swift action over the other points raised in the report. I am certain Munster said much more into Churchill's private ear than was given in his official report to Parliament – the official report only hinted at the true state of affairs suffered by the British soldier out here.

I think you are right, Annie, when you say I will not be happy unless I have a grouse! I usually have one, don't I? Then, there is so much to grouse about, not only about our personal environment out here, and its relatively petty annoyances, but also the larger issues – national and world politics etc. I'm afraid I adopt a very pessimistic and sceptical

Figure 36: Plague warning sign near the Irrawaddy crossing. (© *British Pathé 1149.12: still 58. Reproduced with permission*)

view over our present government. They are forever dishing out fine speeches about liberty, democracy, social security, and the general pure, high-minded motives guiding their policy. But, honestly, don't you think they are just the same breed of addle brained opportunists who have been running things for ages past? I exclude Churchill from the addle brained group – his brain is very clear indeed – which with his strong tendency to despotism makes him the most unscrupulous opportunist of the lot. His increasing refusal to accept even the slightest criticism, added to his recent words and actions in European affairs makes me feel that he is steering us into a nasty mess. And even if we get rid of him after the war I'm quite certain we will be involved in the most awful post war shambles. The only real war aim of Britain is to grab back whatever we have lost through the war in the way of territories and to increase our domination of smaller states. All our fine words on freedom etc. are so much eyewash – you have only to look at our present policy in India to realise that.

Still, post-war chaos or not, I shall be glad to get out of this blasted army and back into a civvy suit. Though I expect I shall be in uniform for another 5 years, for I shall be out here for at least 3 years, and I don't think I'll be demobbed for 2 years after that. And then what –??? Become a medical civil servant, presumably, bound hand and foot with red tape, told where to practice [*sic*], what to give my patients, and generally being messed around. The only advantage, to my mind, such a regimented service will have over the army, is that if I don't like a higher officer I can tell him where to go and what to do with himself – if I did that in the army I would be court-martialled! Oh, the

Figure 37: Tank crossing the Irrawaddy. R. Watson, No. 9 Army Film and Photo Section, Army Film and Photographic Unit. (*IWM SE 3155. Reproduced with permission*)

Figure 38: Mules crossing the Irrawaddy. A. Stubbs, No. 9 Army Film and Photo Section, Army Film and Photographic Unit. (*IWM SE 1858. Reproduced with permission*)

things we do for England!! One thing the army has done for me is to teach me to curb my tongue and only think somebody is a b.f. and not tell him that!

Love,

Harry.

Figure 39: Harry's drawing of a *chinthe*, Myingyan, 1945. (*Author's collection*)

On 1 March, Harry's MSU crossed the Irrawaddy. His division used amphibious vehicles, motor boats and local wooden fishing boats and they swam their mules across. A week later, the division moved out of its bridgehead. Meanwhile, other divisions took Mandalay, the Burmese summer capital at Maymyo, and the river port town of Myingyan.

5. Ind. Mob. Surg. Unit
S.E. Asia Command
13th March 1945

Dear Annie & Flo,

I don't think I acknowledged your letter of Feb. 22nd did I, Annie? And today I got one from you, Flo, dated Feb. 28th, so this will serve as an answer to both of them. I also, the other day, received a big parcel of "Illustrateds"[3] from you, and the parcel of "Motor Cycles" – I suppose the latter are the ones you told me you were getting from the office Flo? I'm still waiting for the book "Riddle of the Sands"!

Thanks for the offer of a book for my birthday, and. I can't think of anything special at the moment – but how about something by Hemingway or Dreiser?[4] I leave the actual book to you.

Yes you <u>can</u> send letters to me for 1½ d now! So don't spend any more sixpences! I got a big letter from Mam today enclosing 2 letters from Aunt Annie[5] and 2 Church letters, total postage 2½ d, and it only took 11 days to come.

Isn't it a pity about Mrs Murchie? She was such a nice person.

Yes I know Barbara Summerfield – a very nice girl. I knew she was pally with a lad in the navy, but it's news that she is engaged to him.

Sorry to hear of all your trouble in the clothes line. Nothing here in Burma to help you out, I'm afraid! Whenever we take a town we have bombed and shelled it to bits before we enter it – no shops left!

Figure 40: Burmese civilian life. Left: returning to Mandalay. (© *British Pathé 1149.12: still 84*) Right: a Burmese house. (© *British Pathé 1821.10: still 40. Reproduced with permission*)

I don't suppose they'll be much of Mandalay left when 19 Div finally capture it all.

I can now tell you that we are with 2nd British Div, and that we have crossed to the south east bank of the Irrawaddy. But I can't give you details following the crossing. I've passed through Kalemyo, Kalewa, Ye-u, and Shwebo – all places you must have heard mentioned on the news. The flying I used to talk about in my letters last December was from Kalemyo to Imphal and back.[6] I can't tell you where we are now – but follow 2 Div's progress on the news, and you will be following my progress at the same time.

I'm tickled at the thought of M'bro having 16 new secondary schools. An excellent plan of Mr Moffett's, but I can't see the niggling town council doing anything about it!

Maybe I <u>was</u> somewhat pessimistic about the duration of my stay out here – my estimates vary with my moods! At the moment I'm feeling cheerful, so I think I'll be out here 3 years, that is just over 18 months more, and demobilised maybe a year after that – say, home by Xmas 1946, and a civvy again by Xmas 1947. It is just 2 years today since I joined the Army – sometimes it seems like two weeks, at others like 20 years!

Your garden sounds very nice, Flo, with all the flowers coming through and it must be much more cheerful to be able to work in a bright sunny office again, after having the windows netted for 5 years.

Well, it's almost lunchtime, so I must finish. It isn't often I can write in the mornings – we don't usually finish work till evening. However (touch wood) it's quiet today, so all being well I'll have a lie down in my tent after lunch, and then go for a swim in the Irrawaddy, and lie and sunbathe on the sandbanks. It's 100° in the shade today – how would you fancy an afternoon in the sun on the riverbank? I bet you'd feel warmish! – coming straight from cold, damp England. I am acclimatised to the heat, after 16 months overseas, so I don't feel it so much.

Cheerio,

Love,

Harry.

Figure 41: Inside Harry's operating tent, March 1945. The lamp reflector is made from a Japanese Zero wing and the clock is from an abandoned Burmese house. He also notes on the back that they were shelled here. (*Author's collection*)

5. Ind. Mob. Surg. Unit
S.E. Asia Command
21st March 1945

Dear Annie & Flo,

At long last your parcel of books, including Mabel's present "Riddle of the Sands", has arrived. It came 3 days ago, but I couldn't acknowledge it before as we were packing up to move. We moved next day (yesterday), set up in our new site, and have been operating today. It's a good place we are in. At one time it seems to have been an R.C. mission. The house is our officers' mess, the church is the reception block and a big two storied building which perhaps was the school now contains the dental centre, pre-op and post op wards and an operating theatre on the ground floor, and the top floor is the surgical unit's sleeping quarters! It's very nice – one big room about 40 yards by 20 for us three officers and our 3 R.A.M.C. men. There's a big R.A.F. bomb crater only 10 yards away so all the windows and doors and half the roof is missing – but that is all to the good as it never rains here until May or June, and we get a cooling breeze through the various holes. Which is very necessary with temperatures of 100 in the shade as we are getting now. The whole site is pleasantly shaded with trees – outside our back windows are some orange trees but the fruit is past its best and a bit dried up. Outside the front of the camp is a lovely straight tarmac road, which is really a sight for sore eyes. After travelling over so many dusty, rutted tracks in our advance to Mandalay it's a treat to see a real road again. The last tarmac I saw was in Imphal – hundreds of miles behind us now.

Yesterday I got another card from you Annie dated Mar. 9. I was very interested to read that Eddie K. was home again. Isn't it typical of our govt. and army that he should be messed around so, after he's given 5 years to the army, 3 of them overseas, and become an invalid because of his service to his country – his grateful country. Nuts!

Thanks for all your efforts to buy in some airmail paper – conditions in the shops sound terrible – what appalling prices your dresses are!

I was tickled to hear of our "stagey" relation – she sounds to be a shocker. One of our relatives we'll prefer to keep dark, I imagine!

I've been looking through the books you sent, and without meaning to be rude at all, I quite agree with you, Ann, that there isn't much choice of literature in the shops. I tried and tried to read one of them called "The man from Manchester",[7] but just couldn't do it! 50 pages finished me – it's just like 19th century melodrama! But one of the others is quite readable, and tomorrow I'll start "R. of the S.". I must write and thank Mabel for that and the cigs.

I don't know who your friend is who has ideas of reform – but I don't think much of her choice of political literature. "The Statesman and Nation"[8] is of course a good periodical, but that thing called "Now" – of all the empty headed trash![9] I'm all for reform, for a little socialism here & there but anyone who can follow the bleating of such an inane, impractical senseless rag must be as potty as the editor of the mag! I read as much of it as I could stomach then threw it away – it seems to result from the infantile brains of a few would be petty intellectuals (so-called) with vague crazy ideas of anarchism. It hasn't even any literary merit! Still, keep sending – it's always thought-provoking if nothing else! I wonder what your friend thinks of these above remarks, after all my revolutionary talk?!!

Must close now. Excuse the patchiness of the writing – I'm dripping sweat all over the paper!

Love, Harry.

Rangoon

During April 1945, the 2nd Division left the Mandalay area for Calcutta to prepare to join a planned amphibious and airborne assault on Rangoon. Again, Harry's unit remained behind, close to the central front, first attached to the 17th Division, then the 5th. 'One gets into a "don't care" frame of mind', Harry wrote. The change of division led, again, to a black mood, and this time with anger directed against Indians in language that is of its time but which is unpleasantly racist today, and which is very different from his earlier opinions about India and Indians.

5. Ind. Mob. Surg. Unit
S.E. Asia Command
2nd April 1945

Dear Annie & Flo,

Excuse pencil, but my pen has gone phut! I've had four communiqués from you today and yesterday. One was one of 2 airgraphs you wrote on Dec. 29th, Ann! I got the other one 2 months ago so where this one has been in the interim I can't think! I also had a very old letter card from you, Flo – written on Jan 3rd. It's that sort of thing that causes unnecessary annoyance and sometimes worry to chaps out here. The mail in general is good, but the Govt. tries to deny that it is ever bad – however these are two examples for you – three months to come. And half of my parcels never arrive at all. When I think of all the cigarettes that I have had sent and the number that arrive!

I also got a card from you, Flo, posted on March 22nd and one from you, Annie, posted on March 20th. They come more rapidly – 11 and

Figure 42: Tanks near Mandalay. E. A. Taylor, No. 9 Army Film and Photo Section, Army Film and Photographic Unit. (*Left: IWM SE 3453. Right: IWM SE 3496. Reproduced with permission*)

13 days respectively. But don't let the Govt. fool you when they say mail is arriving here regularly in a week or 9 days. It isn't. Mine takes 10 to 14 days to arrive.

I laughed at the port which turned out to be water. Yes it was a bit odd receiving a bottle of port from John! Did I tell you I got the motorcycle mags Flo? They were quite enjoyable but I think I must have lost my taste for motorbikes. Yes, the motorcar mags of 1942 and 3 do sound a bit too old.

When you wrote, Flo, things were moving quickly out here. Note I say when you wrote; it must have been interesting reading that bit in News Review[1] – but again, don't let that fool you – they were old and decrepit – further, they were Japanese! They did, as you say, cause us to see red!

But what good does it do? One gets into a "don't care" frame of mind. That's India, the Indian Govt. and the Indian army for you. Bah!!

Now, what makes you think I would be a major, Annie?! I've only had just over 2 years service. Probably if I'd stayed in India and bribed a few Indians and the lousy English officials out here I might be!! It isn't unknown – did the case of Major Dunnette get in the English papers as well as the Indian ones? He got 2 years for taking bribes from officers (mainly Indian) to get them good postings. India – it's made of graft.

About the ointment I gave Auntie Edith – it contained sulphanilamide and cod liver oil, if she wants more.

No, Ann, we still aren't in civilised parts, but on a burnt up parched plain. Though we have passed the odd ruined town.

I am feeling in a bad mood. Hating the army, but hating more so India, and our gallant allies the Indians – the slimy, black faced, filthy, two-faced wogs that they are. Brrh!

Love,

Harry.

The monsoon was due in mid-May and Slim wanted to take Rangoon before then. If this timeline were not met, then the rains would cut supplies to the 14th Army so severely that they might have to retreat to northern Burma. So, during April, the infantry divisions, with trucks, tanks and artillery, leapfrogged each other down narrow north-south corridors along the lines of the railway and the Irrawaddy. They secured airstrips every 50 miles or so and flew in supplies and airborne troops, travelling over 300 miles in three weeks. There were some 77,000 Japanese troops around these corridors, with little transport or supplies but fiercely resisting in groups in villages and on hills. The 14th Army bypassed many of these pockets, leaving them to be 'mopped-up' later. Japanese defenders mined or demolished strategic points and some mounted suicide missions. The British *Official History* records that even patients in a captured Japanese field hospital refused to surrender.

The divisional field ambulances also leapfrogged each other during the advance to Rangoon. Harry's unit appears to have been part of the 17th Indian Division at this time, moving from Meiktila down the railway. Battle casualties were considered 'light', as is confirmed in the chart of daily operations in Figure 23, which covers the 'race to Rangoon' from February to May, 1945. Wounded men were taken to the nearest MSU for treatment and evacuated by air when they were stable. The field ambulance and its MSU then closed and bounded forward again. 5IMSU reached Pegu on 29 April and, on 30 April, they found a party of 250 prisoners-of war, American, British and Indian, who had escaped from captivity in Rangoon.

The monsoon arrived on the same day, two weeks earlier than anticipated, and stopped all air transport and off-road tank and truck movements. The 14th Army was only 50 miles from Rangoon. This meant that Harry's old division, the 2nd, reached Rangoon before he did, as part of the assault from sea and air. The city was taken during the first week in May and the several Army divisions linked up.

The future looked optimistic. VE Day, marking the end of the war in Europe, was on 8 May. Allied prisoners of war were released from Japanese camps. Harry's unit was housed in one of those spacious colonial bungalows surrounded by gardens that have become desirable 'heritage' properties in South-East Asia today. 5IMSU changed divisions again on 9 May, moving from the 17th Division to its old hosts, the 5th.

5. Ind. Mob. Surg. Unit
S.E. Asia Command
6th May 1945

Dear Annie & Flo,

It's a long time since I last wrote to you, but I've been so busy dashing about that I have written no letters at all. Doubtless you will have heard on the B.B.C. the news of the 14th Army's dash south through Burma, culminating in a landing at Rangoon by 15 Corps?

You can imagine that life in 14th Army has been quite hectic of late, and you'll excuse my lack of correspondence I know. With all this moving I have lost most of my mail, having received only one lot in the past month. It included a very welcome parcel of books and cigarettes, and an air letter card from you, Flo.

The books are very readable, and I kept one with me in the cab of my truck to read during the frequent halts. The cigarettes I appreciated very much, as I had none at all. I have finished them now, and am reduced to the ration of 7 Indian De Reskes per day – a punishment I would hardly even wish on Hitler!

Your card of the 20th reached me on 29th of April Flo – quite quick. You are quite right about imagining what I think about our so-called improved amenities – there's an example of how good they are to us just above!

The news is grand now, isn't it? All the Germans surrendered in Italy, Holland, N. Germany. Only a few left now. When you get this it will be all over, I'm sure.

Then on to Japan! We've come a long way out here in our quiet way while Europe has been getting all the publicity. We were reckoning up only yesterday, since I joined this unit last May, we have advanced, with the leading troops, about 900 miles. Think of it! That in itself is about twice as far as they have advanced in Europe.

Figure 43: Liberated prisoners of war, Rangoon area, 1945. Unknown photographer. (*National Archives: WO 361/2045*)

Excuse the blotches – it's not tears or rain – just sweat! It is terribly humid here, though not over hot only about 90°. It has been raining almost without stop for 3 days & nights – real monsoon weather. Thank goodness we have good cover. The whole unit is housed in a lovely European style bungalow. It is white painted, with a large covered porch on which I am writing this. There is a big front garden with some lovely red roses, bougainvillaea, and a yellow flower like honeysuckle. There are two big gates with a drive connecting them curving past the front door.

This town is relatively undamaged, and we are in a row of nice houses, each one in its own grounds. Next door is the officers' mess, and next door the other way the men's mess. The road past us is of lovely smooth tarmac, and across it a large open park of green grass.

Next door in the men's mess are living some British escaped prisoners. They broke loose from the Japs a few days ago just before we captured this town. We took a tooth out for one of them an hour or two ago. He had been a P.O.W. for 3 years, but didn't look unfit. He was very chirpy, and wanted to stay on and fight instead of being repatriated home (he had 9 years service in the East)!

Well, all for now. Hope I hear from you again soon.

Love,

Harry.

Thousands of Japanese troops in Burma were making their way east towards Thailand. The Allies were already making plans to retake Malaya so it was important to Slim to destroy the remaining enemy before they had a chance to reorganise. He ordered patrolling on either side of the Irrawaddy valley and in the Pegu Yomas, a range of hills between the Irrawaddy and Sittang rivers. In the dry phrases of the *Official History*, there was 'stubborn resistance', 'determined opposition', brisk action' and 'severe fighting'.

5. Ind. Mob. Surg. Unit
S.E. Asia Command
22nd May 1945

Dear Annie & Flo,

I've two letters from you in the past two days, Annie, one written on April 17th and the other on V Day.

You seem to have crammed so much news into them that I'll have a job finding space to reply! Although I have no news from this end for you, so that will save space. The war is treating us quietly for the moment, thank goodness. Oh yes, there is still a war on out here! I know the B.B.C. and the papers would hardly give you that impression but rest assured there is still fighting!

The house must look nice after all its painting and distempering. What a pity you can't get decent new curtains to match the new paintwork. Still perhaps things will improve soon, and rationing be eased. Then you'll also be able to get some new clothes you always seem to be short of!

Eddie Knott seems to have landed a nice job. It's very good to hear it. Perhaps it will keep him going until he is demobbed.

Fancy Les Murchie volunteering for service out East! I hope he has no illusions about the glamour of the Orient! He'll soon lose them if he has.

Glad to hear your teeth are settling down now, Ann. I hope they stay that way!

What is the idea of turning these elementary schools into secondary schools? Granted, M'bro needs more secondary school places than were provided by Acklam and the High School. But, surely they don't need several more schools?

Thanks for the parcel you are sending to celebrate V Day. I wonder will it ever arrive? The parcel situation is worse than ever. Someone must be pinching thousands a week. I had a letter from a friend of mine asking if I'd received some Churchman No.1 sent a few months ago. Of course I haven't, nor have I received a Xmas parcel of cigarettes from the same source.

I laughed at your remark, Ann, – "You are seeing the sights, aren't you." What sights? Mandalay? That looks something like the bombed parts of Newport[2] – not much of a sight. Burma? Just flat un-ending plains of either mud or dust – nothing there to call sights. Last year the hills was certainly a sight worth seeing. But I can't think of anything else in India or Burma I want to see again. Except of course Agra and the Taj Mahal.

The so-called colourful people of India and Burma are certainly a "sight". A nauseating one. The more I see of these black devils the more I praise the Lord I'm white and wish I were home with white people again. Greasy, slimy, flea bitten, dirty, shifty beggars all of them.

Something had happened to change the liberal attitudes Harry had expressed while he read Nehru into the insulting descriptions of Indians and Burmans in this letter. In the same letter, he also implies that the Japanese are not 'civilised', unlike the Germans, a contrast to his earlier assessment of them as fine soldiers. But in his next letter he criticises Beverley Nicholls' book, *Verdict on India*, which disparaged Indian society and was dismissive about its religions, especially Hinduism. It is notable that Harry thought the book was destructive and 'one-sided' so soon after he had written racist comments. Later on, the sentiments expressed in the letters become more liberal again, and this instability in his views suggests that the apparent racism was not a fixed opinion but depended on his environment, his stress level, and mood.

V Day seems to have been pretty lively around Tollesby Road, singing in the streets, bonfires, etc. Makes me feel quite envious! I shall have no celebrations (like everyone else out here) until Japan is beaten. Which I'm afraid won't be for a long time, judging by the don't care attitude of the government and population at home. The Jap is a tougher nut than the German, don't forget. Even though Burma is officially conquered, there's still thousands of them fighting here. They won't surrender as would a German or any other civilised person when cut off. But have to be killed to the last man. Which means more of our chaps die. And this will be repeated everywhere we fight the Japs. Look at how they fight in Okinawa. They still are fighting in New Guinea and the Philippines even though they've been hopelessly cut off for ages.

Writing again later,
Love,
Harry.

At the end of May the Allied land forces were reorganised to facilitate the invasion of Malaya and Harry's unit became part of the 12th Army. The Allied role in much of Burma was now restricted to keeping law and order, patrolling to capture or destroy isolated bands of Japanese stragglers only when the Burmese informed on them. But there were still large concentrations of Japanese in the Pegu hills in the east of the country.

5. Ind. Mob. Surg. Unit
S.E. Asia Command
30th May 1945

Dear Annie & Flo,

Just a few lines to acknowledge 2 more cards from you which came the other day. One was a very old one from you, Ann, written on March 31st when you were at Thrumpton. The other, from you Flo, was written on May 15th.

I think the story you tell, Flo, of Gen. Patton thinking the Japs will be finished this year is just too optimistic for words. If you notice, all these tales about the early defeat of Japan come from people who have never fought the little devils. The men out here never make prophecies – they merely say it will be a hard struggle, but hope (and only hope) that it will be shorter now the European war is over. You see the trouble is that they never surrender. Unlike the Germans and Italians or ourselves. If Europeans are cut off and in a hopeless position they surrender to avoid useless waste of life. As we did at Tobruk, the Americans in the Philippines and other examples. But take the Japs –. They've never surrendered anywhere. Cut off in New Guinea for over a year, they still fight. They hold out in the Philippines though they know they have no hope of escape. 12,000 of them are hopelessly cut off here in Burma but they won't surrender. They will either sneak out to Siam in ones and twos or we'll kill them. And that I think is the way it will be everywhere we meet Japs. It means a longer war and more casualties for us, but we kill them out here at the rate of 20 or more to one of ours. By the time the Jap war is finished there shouldn't be many of the yellow baskets left – which suits me. Time was when I looked on them as just other human beings, and felt sorry for them when they were brought in sick and wounded. We gave them good operative attention, as good as our own chaps got.

In the past year we have changed our views. We in this unit don't operate on Japs unless they present a surgically interesting or unusual case.[3] Which makes it that we haven't touched one for 6 months. Let the – s rot, I say. Why should I devote such time & skill as I might have to these sub-human fiends? The infantry of 2 Div. to whom we were attached had the right idea – they shot all their prisoners. The only ones we ever saw were the odd ones they were ordered to keep alive for interrogation. When we were in 17 Div, the Gurkhas had the right idea too – they slit their throats with a kukri (the big Gurkha killing knife) or cut off their heads – no prisoners. You'll maybe have noticed that 14th Army has killed about a 100,000 Japs (in <u>one year</u>) – but only taken less than 1,000 prisoners?[4] That's the way to do it! Less of them to cause trouble after the war!

I laughed at your account of Dad taking M & D[5] to the station in the car. Just like our cars, wasn't it?!

Your list of books is <u>very</u> interesting, Annie. I've read "Verdict on India", and was surprised that a reputable novelist like Nicholls could write such a book.[6] Many of his facts are true – but it's a one-sided book, completely devoid of constructive criticism – merely destructively critical for the sake of destruction.

If you can get it, how about "Fiesta" by Hemingway, or "An American Tragedy" by Dreiser?

All for now,

Love,
Harry.

No, I didn't see the town on the Irrawaddy with all the pagodas – I forget its name, was it Pagau?[7] I was round Mandalay then and came straight down through Meiktila on the Rangoon road.

There were no major actions during June but the Japanese mounted a local counter-offensive towards Rangoon across the Sittang river which did not end until early July.

5. Ind. Mob. Surg. Unit
S.E. Asia Command
11th June 1945

Dear Annie & Flo,

Still in the same old place as when I last wrote, still having a minimum of work. Life could be reasonably pleasant if it weren't for the continual damp heat. Food is plentiful and good – tons of ducks, chickens, beef, fresh vegetables, and fruit (bananas, mangoes, limes, jackfruit, etc.). Also plenty of cigarettes and drink (beer, whisky, gin & brandy). Better stop before I make you jealous! Rationing at home seems to be stiffer than ever before by all reports. Why don't they let you have decent food and let the continent fend for itself? They should be accustomed to low diet by now after 5 years of German occupation!

Answering your letter, Flo – of June 2, which came yesterday. As far as I know, I don't get the chance to vote as I'll be on the new electoral roll which doesn't come into effect till later in the year. Churchill, by forcing an election now has disenfranchised everyone like myself who has become 21 since the last roll was made 10 years ago. He is showing himself in his true colours now – after praising socialism in Russia for 4 years, he now descends to guttersnipe phrases to describe British socialists. He is a great war leader, but I hope to God he never gets a hand in the peace. The petty bickerings and name-callings between the parties make me sick – obviously the war out here can go hang for all they care. If they don't buck up and get things done out here, get more men out east, reduce repatriation etc, they'll have a mutiny. Chaps here are comparing our far east war effort unfavourably with the Americans', who have already started sending one army from Germany and one from Italy out here. They (the Yanks) said weeks ago they were sending 7,000,000 men east – we have done nothing. To my mind we don't intend doing anything – we will sit back (by we I mean the govt.) and let the Yanks finish the Japs, and keep the chaps already out here, out here for years more. But, as I said before, the British government does what the British people want and the people being just so many dumb cattle express no opinion at all. The fighting spirit of Britain!! What a country. Sometimes I think the Dominions and U.S.A. are the only live communities in this world. They certainly are more virile and go ahead than that den of sloth and smug self-satisfaction we call Great (?!) Britain.

You say, Flo, that you don't associate red roses and good roads with India. Who said I was in India? I crossed into Burma one year ago, and have been here ever since. Burma, BURMA, BURMA!!!! India is a land of peace, where all the gun shy base wallahs live. They live a better life there than you do in England. War is in BURMA! I'm not criticising you, Flo, but that's something that annoys men out here – the lack of information at home about the war out here. After all the fighting here for years, folks at home are still ignorant of the facts of this front. I read in an English paper, only a month old, an account of Mountbatten visiting British war cemeteries here. The photo showed him (as the paper said) visiting a cemetery at Garrison Hill in Arakan. Most folks at home, of course, never heard of either Garrison Hill or Arakan. Garrison Hill is in Kohima, and there thousands of men of 2nd British Div were wiped out a year ago stopping the Jap invasion of India. I was 30 miles from there at the time. Arakan is a thousand miles from Garrison Hill, and was a different campaign altogether!

Your 6d collection for your next V Day celebrations will be on ice for a long time yet. I bet the Japs won't be finished for at least 2 more years – even if the Yanks invade Japan itself before then. I'm very pessimistic about the war out here. Even if Britain did her best it would be a hard and long struggle, and obviously Britain is not doing her best. They've even stopped calling up men of 30, while there are chaps of 35, 40, and more still out here.

Love,

Harry.

Snakes, Cigarettes and Weddings

5. Ind. Mob. Surg. Unit
S.E. Asia Command
12th June 1945

Dear Annie & Flo,[1]

When I wrote yesterday acknowledging Flo's letter of June 2nd, I forgot to acknowledge Annie's of May 24th which came a week ago. So here's another letter from me – you lucky people!!

You're quite right, Ann, I wouldn't mind sampling your weather – changeable though it is! Here it is hot and sticky all the time. It rains heavily part of every day, which cools things down momentarily. Everything is damp and will not dry – our clothes, the bedding is absolutely sodden, and green mould grows on everything from tent poles to boots.

The rain brings out the snakes, and I've seen about 10 killed here in the past 2 weeks ranging from ones 2 feet long to beggars as thick as my wrist and 8 feet long. Brrh! Nasty!

Had a trip into Rangoon the other day. It's a lovely city, fine wide roads with trees along the pavements, and the main roads have a grass strip 12 feet wide all down the centre to form dual carriageways. The docks took our fancy particularly, and we ate our sandwiches (fried egg ones) on the quayside watching the busy scene of steamers unloading and small craft busying about the river, wishing we could have boarded one of the steamers to come home!

This letter has a particularly extensive discussion about the supply and quality of cigarettes, but he mentions them in most of his letters. The

Figure 44: Troops sightseeing in Rangoon. L. W. Marshall, No. 9 Army Film and Photo Section, Army Film and Photographic Unit. (*IWM SE 4108. Reproduced with permission*)

dangers of smoking were not appreciated at this time and Harry was a heavy smoker from his teens. After the War he signed up for Richard Doll's study of smoking and health, which recruited a large cohort of British doctors. Harry's was one of the earlier deaths during the follow-up phase of the research, from a heart attack.[1] It is ironic to read in these letters so many references to smoking. The War helped to kill him, but indirectly.

> I'm surprised at what you say, Ann, of Montgomery asking for 2 million more cigs for his men. Surprise that he asked for so few! For he must have almost 2 million men, which only gives them 1 each!

When you read about us in Burma getting more just wink to yourself and say "nuts"! We are given a ration of 50 cigs a week free (same as in Europe). But they aren't the English ones they get in Europe – they're Indian Woodbines and De Reskyes [*sic*]. I know the De Rs in England are foul but these Indian ones are unbelievable, they have nothing in common but the name. Sometimes (like last month) we get even worse ones, like Lions, Vs, etc. Officially they are forbidden to be issued to British troops – but they give us them anyway. They are so bad the sepoys won't touch them (and they usually smoke any damn thing!)

However in the past 2 weeks things have improved, and we have been able to supplement our ration with Indian Players bought from the canteen. We also got 2 months liquor ration (April and May) last week, so I had 2 bottles of Black & White whisky, 2 bottles of Booth's gin, 1 bottle of Portuguese brandy, 5 quart bottles of American beer and 7 half pint bottles of American beer! Like some?!

As for the increased cigarette ration of 100 cigarettes weekly made from American tobacco, that Churchill three months ago promised we should get in June – we've never seen that and don't expect to. It's more Govt. eyewash to quieten the public at home. Same as the latest announcement that repatriation is down to 3 years 4 months. Why, they can't even get everyone away when they've done 3 yrs 8 mths. So 3y 4m means nothing at all. There have been men killed near here in the past few days who'd done 3 yrs 7 months and thereabouts. Do you blame us out here for being cynical and bitter at every announcement the Govt. makes? We have no reason to be otherwise. The Govt. makes a promise, everyone at home is happy, then no efforts are made to implement the promise. It happens again and again. And it isn't just the Tories' fault. Labour and Liberal are to blame, too. In fact the whole British public – that stolid, bovine mass of clods.

Love,

Harry.

[I've no remarks to make about Mary's latest engagement. Yes, weddings <u>are</u> coming fast, but not mine, thank God. I've got more serious things to do for a few years than rush into things as some folks have done and are going to do.]

This 'not mine' remark is the only reference in the letters to his girlfriend, Margaret Wallace, and none of the wartime letters between them have survived. Margaret joined Queen Alexandra's Royal Naval Nursing Service (QARNNS) in 1942, one of over 1,000 civilian nursing sisters who joined the QARNNS during the War. When Harry left for India in 1943, she was based at the temporary naval hospital in Kingseat, Aberdeenshire. She travelled to Ceylon in March-April 1944 at the same time as Mountbatten moved the SEAC Headquarters from Delhi to Kandy in Ceylon, and just as Harry was seconded to work at 66IGH in support of Kohima.

It was an anxious time for those waiting for news of convoys in the Indian Ocean, where Japanese submarines were active. They sank 385 Allied ships there during the War. Margaret's convoy was the one which followed the ill-fated Convoy KR8 from Kilindini to Colombo.[2] The troopship SS *Khedive Ismail* was hit by a torpedo from submarine *I-27*. The ship sank within minutes, the submarine hid beneath floating survivors, and many were killed by depth charges dropped by British destroyers. Amongst the over 1,000 lives lost were 77 Army nursing sisters and women from the Women's Royal Naval Service, the greatest loss of life amongst female Commonwealth service personnel during the War.[3]

Ceylon was an offensive base and 'seething with the military', packed with soldiers, sailors and airmen from many nations, as well as journalists, spies and the miscellany who transit through wartime headquarters.[4] Margaret worked at two naval hospitals during her two years in Colombo. A photograph of her in white tropical uniform, surrounded by smiling staff and patients, suggests that although the work was busy, it was carried out in a relaxed atmosphere far removed from the mud and flies of Harry's tents and bunkers in Burma.

Harry's off-duty time was occupied with writing letters and reading, and Christmas dinner, 1944, was 'just a marquee with food & drink on tables – help yourself, no service'. Ceylon, in contrast, was a playground for the young military personnel posted there, with excursions to palm-fringed beaches, sightseeing tours round the island's ancient royal and religious sites, exciting trips on a vertiginous railway line to tea plantations

Figure 45: Sister Margaret Wallace with her staff and patients, Colombo, 1944–5. (*Author's collection*)

in the hills, and shopping expeditions in the bazaars. The island's tropical beauty captivated its visitors.[5] The few women in the services were much in demand as dance partners and as companions on outings and they worked and played hard. One naval nursing assistant, in Ceylon for two years at the same time as Margaret, describes 'nothing but a crazy round of laboured routine, nothing but a gay whirl of synthetic parties [and a] clammy, light-headed blare of night clubs'.[6] The family photograph collection includes one of Margaret on a beach looking glamorous in a halter top and large sunhat. Harry also went on swimming expeditions, but in rivers near burning ammunition dumps or plague warnings. Little wonder he groused in his letters about the delivery of mail and the quality of the cigarettes.

Figure 46: A beach excursion in Ceylon, 1944–6. (*Author's collection*)

5. Ind. Mob. Surg. Unit
S.E. Asia Command
20th June 1945

Dear Annie & Flo,

Your letter posted on June 12th arrived the day before yesterday, and. I think 6 days is the fastest any mail has reached me yet. The average time is about 10 days. I see someone in the Govt. said mail reached India in 4 days, so that allowing for distribution it reached forward troops in 1 week from home on an average. That announcement, like most remarks of the Govt. about things out here, is so much poppycock. A week or so is the best time – average is 10 days or more. And for parcels 2 - 3 months or more – if they arrive at all.

Thanks very much for the parcel you have sent off. Don't bother about books – anything will do. Although reading matter is short here, we can usually scrounge something.

I read the other day in the paper that the Govt. have announced that 100 cigarettes a week ration (free) would be given to the forward troops out here after the middle of June. That's an advance on Churchill's statements of a few months ago – he said they hoped to do it. Well, it's after mid June now, and we are as far forward as anyone here, being part of a division that is actually in action against the Japs – but have we seen the 100 fags yet? Of course not! That's just another bit of political hoo hah for home consumption.

I see the Express correspondent makes quite a song of the fact that Naafi in Rangoon is selling to 14th Army troops. He didn't say that they only sold to us for 2 days! As you know, Naafi isn't allowed in India or Burma – we have to buy from private contractors' canteens (when they are available). They are government controlled but the prices are terrible, and the goods trash. Still, I see Naafi have said that anywhere else we go (and I suppose that means Malaya, Java, Siam etc.) there will be Naafis.

I laughed at the thought of Bert Ensoll presiding at the anniversary! He's a fine upstanding pillar of the church isn't he?!

About the films – I have had one developed, the other is still in the camera. I can't get prints till I go on leave, which I hope will be next month. The developed spool is almost all over-exposed – I haven't allowed sufficiently for the hard glare of the tropical sun. However, such prints as are successful I will send on. So if I do get leave next month, you should have the snaps in August. So far, however, we haven't been told whether we can have leave, never mind when we can have it. It's 2 years in September since I last had any leave – that was my embarkation leave.

Sorry to hear uncle Matt isn't so well. I hope his holiday at Seascale will buck him up.

What exams. are they that Mary's fiancé is taking? Navy or civil exams? What is he in civil life?

From your description of Flo's efforts with the lard ration you will both be growing sleek and fat! I don't think!

Well it's 9 a.m. now, and time I was doing my round on the ward. I'm temporarily running the British ward of the field ambulance as they have no British M.O. of their own to do it. It makes a nice change from anaesthetics, and fills the time in now that there is so little to do in the operating line.

All for now,

Love,

Harry.

After two years without leave, dive-bombed in the Mediterranean, shelled in Burma, repeatedly changing division, opening up for surgery, dealing with a rush of casualties, then closing the unit down again, and always longing for home and civilian life, Harry was finally granted leave for the month of July 1945. A few days after his next letter he went to Darjeeling, the old hill station close to the border with Sikkim at 6,000ft in the Himalayan foothills. He had studio portraits taken for family and friends and took photographs of Everest. On the way back he stayed with his schoolboy cycling companion Jack Blackburn in the steel town of Burnpur in Bengal. Jack was one of those old boys whose work in outposts of Empire might well have been noted in the *News* section of the Middlesbrough High School magazine.

5. Ind. Mob. Surg. Unit
S.E. Asia Command
29th June 1945

Dear "Stolid Ones"!,

I've just (last night) received your letter of June 22nd, Ann, signed "one of the stolid mass of bovine clods"!!

Honestly, it gave me the best laugh I've had for some time. My letter to which it was a reply must have contained some outrageous statements! You sound very righteously indignant, Ann!

But you know by now not to take all my utterances at their face value – some of them need a bucket full rather than a pinch of salt!

Figure 47: On the road to Darjeeling. Wartime postcard. Unknown photographer. (*Author's collection*)

Nevertheless you must make allowances for some of my more exuberant phrases – we out here do get a trifle wild occasionally when we read of all the petty, political squabbles at home. Churchill's statements about the Labour party are particularly sickening – saying they aren't fit to govern, that they'll take all our savings, and impose secret police on us. Did you ever hear such nonsense? He seems to forget that these same Labour men formed part (a very large part) of his government that beat Germany. He forgets that politically they represent the mass of the workers who produce the arms that made victory possible. And his filthy remarks about socialism sounded strangely out of place with his professed admiration and friendship for Russia, and his eulogistic remarks about Russia when that country was bearing the brunt of German attacks.

I see the United Nations at San Francisco have produced their manifesto – and very fine and noble it sounds, too. How on earth can the British people expect a man like Churchill to work for future world peace in such a scheme, in harmony with Russia, when he is obviously violently against all elementary principles of democracy?

I've said many times that Churchill is a fine war leader (so was Rommel for that matter!) But as a peacetime politician he is a perpetual menace. To use his own words – "put him out to grass". He's done a fine job – let us honour him for it, and pension him off.

Even worse than Churchill are the Conservative Party – representatives of vested interests. They have no interest in you and me, the common people. Money is their one idol. Social improvement and advancement, domestic and national, means nothing to them. Profit is everything.

But can you get the average man or woman to see that? Can the bulk of our population see further than the ends of their noses? No! They are blind to all important things – they believe anything and everything the Daily Mail or the Express want them to believe and allow themselves to be led around like pet animals – the ignorant fools! That's why I call them a "stolid mass of bovine clods" (no personalities intended – it's a generality) – just a stodgy mass of politically unread, patient chuckleheads. So long as they can get their pint of beer, visit the pictures, dogs, or football match – what does the average man care about the running of the country? Nothing!

You are right about our booze ration, it really is very good – more than I can drink, but of course I'm very abstemious.

Thanks for the birthday parcel – I'm looking forward to its arrival. Please don't bother about soap – I can get Lux or Lifebuoy (Indian made but good – made in Lever's Indian factory) as much as I want in the canteen. As for shaving soap, I have more than I can use – I still have 4 or 5 sticks I bought in England before I left, amongst others.

I get angry when I think of your reduced rations and can't see the need for it. But I've raved on that point in previous letters to home and to you.

Yes, I, like many others of my acquaintance here, have toyed with the idea of emigration after the war, not very seriously I admit. But if we are to be governed by the same old Tory gang I might consider it more earnestly.

Surprised to hear your remarks re Jews, Ann – don't forget it's the capitalist Jews that are the bad ones – capitalism is the operative word, not Jew! Love, Harry. XX

On 19 July between 16,000–19,000 Japanese set out from the Pegu hills to cross the Sittang river and reach Thailand. Bullock carts were their only transport and they foraged for food. Between one and two thousand, too weak to march, were left behind in the hills to die. The Allies had received prior intelligence about this break-out and it was opposed. It is estimated that by 4 August no more than 4,000 to 5,000 Japanese had reached the east bank of the Sittang to escape. 'Yet the question of surrender did not arise.'

Figure 48: The studio photograph taken in Darjeeling, July 1945. (*Author's collection*)

5. Ind. Mob. Surg. Unit
S.E. Asia Command
2nd August 1945

Dear Annie & Flo,

I'm writing this from Calcutta, where I am held up waiting for a boat to take me back to my unit. I'm staying in a very nice club on Chowringhee, Calcutta's main street. I've been here a couple of days and have spent my time looking round the shops mainly. I went out last night and the night before with two M.O.s from my old unit 21 B.G.H., and yesterday afternoon I went to the flicks to see Walt Disney's "Gay Caballeros" – quite funny, with Donald Duck having terrific adventures in South America.

Last week I spent at Jack Blackburn's place in Burnpur. Had a nice quiet time. His wife and family are in Darjeeling, and Jack was on night shift (11-7), so I had the house to myself. We bathed every morning or evening in a lovely open air pool which is only a couple of minutes from Jack's bungalow.

It's terribly sticky here in Calcutta, though it's not quite so hot as it was when I arrived a month ago on my way to Darjeeling. And it rained heavily last night, which cooled things down and freshened the atmosphere.

Have you got over the surprise of the election yet??! It was an amazing vote wasn't it? It was obvious that the whole country was going Left, particularly the younger generation and chaps in the forces, and that everyone was fed up with the Tories. But I expected them to get in by a narrow margin with Churchill at their head.

However, Labour are very much in power, and we'll have to wait and see how they shape. I don't expect them to perform miracles, and they will undoubtedly make many blunders – any post war government is bound to in clearing up the mess caused by the war. At least, even if they do their worst, they cannot do a worse job than the Tories, thank the Lord!

And they have the opportunity of doing a lot of real good – especially in foreign affairs. Though I can't see Ernie Bevin as Foreign Minister! He should have stuck to the Ministry of Labour.

You'll be a Civil Servant soon, Flo, if they nationalise the steel industry![7] Just as I will be when they nationalise medicine! Anyway, civil servants have an easy job – drink tea all day, good holidays and a pension – ask Mary and Margaret and Marion! Almost as good a job as a schoolteacher's – what do you say, Ann?! 5 or 6 hours work a day, 5 days a week, with 2 months holiday a year – money for jam! Alright, Ann, I'll duck while you throw the kitchen stove at me!!

Writing again when I get back to the unit – in about a week, I hope.

Love,

Harry.

On 6 August the first atomic bomb destroyed Hiroshima. On 9 August the second fell on Nagasaki. On 12 August, Japan surrendered.

Figure 49: Chowringhee in Calcutta in wartime. (*Clyde Waddell collection, University of Pennsylvania. Creative Commons Public Domain*)

Harry had been away from the War for a month. After letter after letter containing tense, angry, cynical and pessimistic comments – we would call him burned-out today – he sounds himself again on his return from leave in August, relaxed, thoughtful and interested in what is around him.

5. Ind. Mob. Surg. Unit
S.E. Asia Command
10th August 1945

Dear Annie & Flo,

When I got back to the unit 3 days ago there were quite a few letters from you both waiting for me. From you, Ann, there were 3 cards, written on July 16th, 21st and 1st, and from you Flo, 2 cards, written on 27th and 28th July. Then yesterday another card dated July 30th came from you, Ann. Thanks for all the mail.

I had a good trip back – by air. And as a result I am here before our surgeon Ives, who left 2 or 3 days before me, by sea. We've got a new surgeon just arrived, Gordon, who was with the B.L.A.[8] with a surgical unit.

The weather here is pleasantly cool after Calcutta, but it rains almost incessantly. We are doing no work, just resting and taking stock and re-organising ready for any future "do's". Our sergeant is just sweating on the top line for his repat. He's done 3 yrs 6 months, and expected to go this month, but now we learn he won't go till next month. Ives also will be going soon as he has about the same length of overseas service.

I now own a jeep! At least the unit does, but I'm M.T.O. (motor transport officer), so it's my baby. It's second hand, but in good shape. I just took [it] into workshops a few minutes ago to have its headlamps fixed.

Having explained one abbreviation I shall elucidate the ones you ask about, Ann. Con. Depot means Convalescent Depot – where chaps are sent after a long illness or wounds, to be trained back into shape for fighting again. A.D.M.S. means Assistant Director of Medical Services. In a division he is the boss M.O. and holds the rank of a full colonel.

He controls all the unit M.O.s, the field ambulances, hygiene section, and any attached units – like ours. D.A.D.M.S. is Deputy A.D.M.S. – a major, who is the A.D.M.S's stooge, and usually runs the A.D.M.S. office at Division H.Q.

You see, the biggest noise in the Army medical services is the D.G.A.M.S. (Director-General of Army Medical Services). He at the moment is Lieut General Sir Alan Hood. He hangs out at the War Office. Under him are chaps called D.M.S. (Director of Medical Services) (major general) one for a group of armies – we have one for S.E.A.C. Under them are the D.D.M.S.'s (Deputy Directors) (brigadier) of the individual armies. Then D.D.M.S.'s (same thing) of corps, then A.D.M.S. of the divisions in the corps. – All clear now?!

I had a letter from Mary D. yesterday telling me all about her cycling tour in the Highlands – it sounded a lovely trip. I wish I could have seen "Merrie England" with you & Mam, Flo. It must have been a fine show. I'm glad you like my photo. It's a pity it got creased – Mam & Dad's copy did too. Anyway it can sit on your gramophone and keep an eye on you till the original gets back! I hope the rationing improves before then – I'll eat all your rations for a week if I come for one supper, at present amounts!

Glad to hear your fruit farm is at last in full production – a pity the four apples were swiped!

The parcels haven't arrived yet, but you know from previous letters of mine how many get through. Why the Govt. don't tighten the postal services up I don't know. Anyone caught pinching parcels should be put back in the army and sent to the unit for which the parcel he pinched was destined – that would discourage the thieves!

Thank you for your birthday greetings. What do you think of the latest war developments? With Russia declaring war, and the Americans using their atomic bomb, I wonder if the Japs will surrender this year? I hope so. Maybe in that event you will be able to give my next birthday greetings in person! Though I am still banking on being home about next November – about 1 year and 3 months from now. It should pass quite quickly.

Well, that's all for now, so I will close. Writing later.
Love,
Harry.

From today's perspective, Harry is surprisingly matter-of-fact about the atomic bombs. He brackets their use with the Russian declaration of war on Japan and it is all part of the endless speculations about when the Japanese might surrender. The public appetite for nuclear disarmament did not take off until after Harry's death and many memoirs of the time record the troops' happiness at the news of the atomic bombs. Paddy Donaldson remembers training for a projected amphibious landing in Malaya when his clambering in and out of landing craft was interrupted by 'a sudden burst of gunfire followed by explosions from weapons of all shapes and sizes. After a day of rumours, it had been confirmed, with ensuing jubilation, that powerful bombs had been dropped on Japan, which would now surrender.'

Singapore

During August 1945, there were still about half a million Japanese troops in Malaya, Singapore, Thailand, Indochina,[1] the Dutch East Indies[2] and Hong Kong. These forces were intact and unbeaten and it was unclear if they would obey instructions to surrender. The American General MacArthur ordered that no entry should be made to these territories until after the formal surrender, which took place in Tokyo Bay on 2 September. There were many thousands of civilian internees, forced labourers and military prisoners-of-war, of many nationalities, held in camps throughout the Japanese-held territories, often in harsh conditions. The relief effort was held up because of the delay in agreeing terms on the formal surrender so Allied planes dropped leaflets and supplies over the camps. Supply ships were dispatched in advance of the surrender and troops, with medical units, were deployed after the surrender.

On 28 August Harry's unit was 'on a ship, waiting to go to "I-know-where-but-can't-tell-you"!!' This was Singapore, where the formal surrender of the Japanese Army, Southern Regions, would eventually take place on 12 September. *Dilwarra*, the troopship on which Harry travelled, later became the SEAC headquarters ship during the surrender process.

5. Ind. Mob. Surg. Unit
S.E. Asia Command
28th August 1945

Dear Annie & Flo,

I got some mail today, the first for about 2 weeks, including a card from you, Ann, written at Barrow on V. J. 2.

Figure 50: SS *Dilwarra*. *Shipping Today and Yesterday* collection. (*Reproduced with permission*)

As I said in my last letter home we are on a ship, waiting to go to "I-know-where-but-can't-tell-you"!! Our mail till today has been directed, I think, to c/o another unit on a different ship, and we'll have to wait till the other end of the voyage to collect it.

Yes, it was good news – VJ Day – wasn't it? But we didn't celebrate it. We celebrated the night we heard the Japs were ready to surrender. It took so long for the govt. to decide whether to accept their conditions about the emperor or not, that the actual VJ day passed without incident.

Altogether I think we are being too soft with those yellow b – s. Discussion after discussion, putting up with the Japs' excuses for delay. MacArthur doesn't seem to be standing much nonsense but is telling them exactly what to do. But we in S.E.A.C. seem, by radio reports, to be allowing the Japs to pull the wool over our eyes by their delaying tactics, and prolonged talks. Mark my words, these b – Japs will pull a fast one if they can. They look on their surrender as only a temporary setback – witness their emperor's speech. The trouble is that, unlike Germany, Japan hasn't been decisively beaten in the field, and they still have all their fanatical fighting spirit left. The only thing to do with them is to kill plenty of them and humiliate them, from the emperor down.

Most of the folks here that I have spoken to are pessimistic as to our future with Japan. Consensus of opinion is that unless we are tremendously careful we'll have another Japanese war before long. I only hope we are very careful!

I expect, at least I hope!, that victory will hasten my return home. I have a hope that I'll be home in a year's time. But we are all very disappointed indeed at the Labour Govt's release plans. Only up to group 23 by the end of the year. They have already released 16 groups. So that means only 7 groups in the next 4 months – approximately 2 groups per month. I am group 46. At that rate I won't be out till the end of 1946! – at the earliest. Let's hope they'll speed it up.

Well, I'm on the move again. Sorry I can't say where to – maybe I shall be able to tell you at the other end.

It certainly looks as though my Xmas forecast last year will be true – Xmas 1946 at home amongst other things.

As I write, the ship's amplifier system is relaying a B.B.C. broadcast of a test match v Australia from London! Amazing, to think of cricket as we sweat here in this sticky Burmese river!

Closing now to get this in in time to catch the mail launch tomorrow morning.

Love,
Harry

The Allied forces were reorganised and SEAC was enlarged. During September and October, the 12th Army, which took over from the 14th Army, moved off to the various Japanese-held countries and switched from waging war to a humanitarian mission: peacekeeping, releasing and repatriating internees and prisoners, and disarming and repatriating the Japanese.

5. Ind. Mob. Surg. Unit
S.E. Asia Command
17th September 1945

Dear Annie & Flo,

I'm writing this on one of your presents! I've received, today and yesterday, about 2 dozen parcels (2 dozen if I include bundles of papers etc.) and amongst them were some from you. I got your birthday parcels no 1 and no 2, and the cake was lovely, Flo – thank you very much. I also got another parcel from you dated May 31st, with the book and cigs enclosed from Mabel. Please give her my best wishes and my very grateful thanks won't you?

Although I'm naturally very pleased at receiving all these parcels, it does make me annoyed. They must have been held up somewhere for months, then all delivered together. So that now I have so many books and magazines I don't know which to start first. If they had been delivered correctly I should have had a parcel every few days for months back.

I have more cigarettes than I can smoke! Just before these parcels arrived I bought 500 in the canteen, and now I've received those in your parcels plus 3 duty free parcels of cigs! I think you'd better stop buying cigarettes for me – they are in such short supply in England and also expensive. And my duty free ones seem to be arriving better now. Those I buy from the canteen are quite smokeable – Indian Players at 20 for 10d. Also, at the moment while we are still on composite rations,[3] we get an issue free, of 12 English Gold Flake per day, of which I get 2 men's ration (24 cigs) – Gordon's and my own. So you can see I have more fags than I can smoke for months to come!

Although I have received all these parcels, letters are conspicuous by their absence. Today I had a card from you, Ann, written at Barrow on Aug 23rd but that is the only letter from England I've had since we sailed from Rangoon. I suppose we'll get a flood of letters, too, one of these days!

I must try to get Aunt Edith a photo of myself, but unfortunately I have lost the address of the photographer in Darjeeling. Will you look it up on your copy, also the number on the back of the photo if possible, and let me have it?

I hope the films Aunt Edith was posting will arrive soon, for I have none at all, and there are some nice views in Singapore, and interesting street scenes.

I laughed when you asked had I seen any Jap prisoners! We naturally didn't see many in Burma – live ones, that is, as we killed most of them. But here there are tens of thousands, though they are rapidly being cleared off Singapore island, and the only ones left are used as labour gangs. There are also lots of I.N.A. (Indian National Army) – Indians who went over to the Japs. I inspected 4 of their camps 2 days ago where there were 3000 of them.

We are quite enjoying life now, doing no surgical work, but quite busy in other ways. For the past few days we have been sorting out our unit doing inventories of everything we have, and collecting worn out equipment together to return it to salvage. Today we've been repainting and numbering all our boxes and panniers. Tomorrow

Figure 51: Colonial bungalow in Singapore. One of many. (*© Lee Kip Lin and the National Library Board, Singapore. Reproduced with permission*)

Gordon and I are taking old stuff down into town to medical stores, and we're going to look round the bazaars while we are there to see what there is in the silk line.

We are living in a lovely house, upstairs on a wide balcony. There is electric light, ceiling fans, an electric refrigerator, and a radio. We have looted tons of armchairs, tables, carpets, rugs, and cupboards from other houses, so we live in luxury. Each night we can get the B.B.C. on the radio while we sip iced beer or gin and lime, the tinkling of the ice cubes in the glasses harmonising nicely with the music from London and the swishing of the ceiling fans!

Our house stands in about an acre of ground, surrounded by high trees, set back about 50 yards from the main road about 50 feet below us. There is a drive winding up the slope from the road so we can drive right up to the front door. All the houses here are of white plaster, and there are no hedges between them, so it all looks like open parkland.

Our original spot, in Singapore General Hospital, was nice, but this is better. We are 2 miles from the city centre, in what must have been the best residential part. It's nice to wash in a real bathroom again – even if the water only runs from the taps after 8 p.m. – and such luxury to sit on a real seat in the doodah! And pull a plug afterwards!

You will have read in the papers about 5 Div occupying Singapore? That was us. You won't see my picture on the newsreels, as we landed at a different dock from the photographers.

We are all waiting now for an announcement about release. There are so many men out here who will have absolutely nothing to do in a month or two, when the Japs are all in prison camps. Already most of us in the R.A.M.C. do no medical work whatsoever, and the numbers will increase when all the P.W.s have been sent home in the next week or two. So we want to know how long we are to be kept out here doing nothing. I expect to be here almost another year in view of my high release group (46). I'm glad to see the govt. sat on the T.U.C.'s proposal to release now all men at home and in Europe who are doing nothing, irrespective of their release groups. That would have penalised every man out here, and kept him in the army longer simply because he'd had the misfortune to be sent out here.

Must close now,

Love,

Harry.

Thanks again very much indeed for the cake, the cigarettes and the books.

5. I. M. S. U.
6 October 45

Dear Annie & Flo,

In the last few days I've had a letter card from each of you – yours written on Sept 5, Flo, and yours on Sept 16 Ann. Thankyou both.

Not a great deal to report. We are still in our nice house in Singapore, and don't know when we are moving. There have been rumours of moves for weeks now, but no progress seems to have been made.

I was on tour up in Malaya are a week ago, round Malacca, to look at possible new sites for us, but nothing came of it. And yesterday the field ambulance C.O.[4] came back from an even more fruitless search still further north. So we don't know what is to happen to us. I expect we'll move to some lousy hole and live in tents, as all the base wallahs are crowding into Singapore and the chaps who have done the fighting and lived uncomfortably for years will be kicked out of the first decent billets they've had to make room for them.

What do you think of demob. news? I had hoped to be home next August, but now they say only up to group 31 will be out by the end of June. I'm group 46 so I reckon it will be next Xmas before I'm home, at least! This Govt. is as bad as the last one so far. They seem to be making no serious effort to get the shipping to take us home, with the result that tens of thousands of us will rot out here for almost 2 years after the finish of the war. I'm in a high enough group, I know, but think of the lads younger than me, in groups 50 to 60, who've been out here for a year or two already. Lord only knows when they'll get home.

It will be interesting to hear what Lawson has to say about his tour out here. I'll be surprised if he does more than add a few more gallons of mush to the sea of platitudinous utterances the Govt. wallows in

But I'm glad the Govt. sat so promptly on the T.U.C. proposal that troops in England doing nothing be released irrespective of their groups. Why should a chap be kept in the army merely because he is in Burma and a chap in the same group get out because he's at home?

10 Oct. Sorry for the break, but I was suddenly whisked away for a sea trip, and didn't get back till 3 hours ago. In my absence I received a letter from each of you, written on 25th September.

You seem to be doing quite a job in the garden, Flo – it must look much better now the shelter has gone. Though I expect it must look rather forlorn in the cold weather you've been having.

I see in your letter you hold the T.U.C.'s views about release, Ann! Why should a man who has a job to go to get out of the army before another of the same group who has no job to go to? Surely it would be fairer to release the one without a job first, to give him time to look for a job. The one with the job has his job waiting for him whenever he leaves the army, and he will get a very unfair advantage if he is released before his turn. Believe me, if they release chaps at home before those out here there'll be a mutiny in the East – and I'd be willing to take a leading part in it. It's a thing we out here feel very strongly about.

I must cut short as I have to go to sea again tomorrow morning, and must repack.

Love,

Harry.

Surabaya

During the weeks between the atomic bombs and the official surrender, independence movements took power in Indochina and the Dutch East Indies and resisted their former colonial masters, the French and Dutch. Harry's unit did not go to Malaya. Instead it went with the 5th Division to the large port city of Surabaya in Java in the Dutch East Indies.

Figure 52: Nationalist graffiti in Surabaya. No. 9 Army Film and Photo Section, Army Film and Photographic Unit. (*IWM SE 5639. Reproduced with permission*)

In late September 1945, small army detachments arrived in Java only to find that the Dutch former colonists were much resented and that a provisional independence government was well-established, supported by the soldiers of the former colonial army. There were also about 70,000 irregulars on the streets, armed with weapons the Japanese had relinquished, including tanks and mortars. Allied soldiers and Dutch internees were attacked and killed.

Reinforcements arrived in late October and their commander, Brigadier Mallaby, was killed on 30 October while trying to negotiate a ceasefire.

Figure 53: Civilian casualty in Surabaya. No. 9 Army Film and Photo Section, Army Film and Photographic Unit. (*IWM SE 5715. Reproduced with permission*)

Some 400 soldiers were killed or injured in the fighting and there were about 6,000 Indonesian casualties.

The 5th Division, including Harry's unit, occupied Surabaya between 10 and 28 November. The occupation was supported by an air and naval bombardment. Thousands of interned Dutch civilians and Allied prisoners-of-war were evacuated to safety but many Indonesians were killed or wounded during the fighting, the final straw in Harry's disgust with the British government and Empire.

5. I. M. S. U.
S. E. A. C.
24th November '45

Dear Annie & Flo,

I've been very remiss over my correspondence, I'm afraid, but I have a good excuse. We've been working harder for the past 3 weeks than ever we did during the "war". Each day we have operated for at least 12 hours on end, usually more, and at the moment we have done 170 cases – most of them in the last 2 weeks.

Now, however, another surgical unit has moved in alongside us, and we are working 24 hour shifts, so I have a little time to write a letter or two. Not that we do nothing in our 24 hour "off" period – we have to get stuff sterilised for the next day, get the theatre cleaned, catch up with our office work etc, etc. Still, it does make things easier having another team to share the work.

I've had one or two letters from you both in the past two weeks – one from you Flo, dated 23rd Oct, and 3 from you, Ann, dated 22nd, 29th Oct, and 4th Nov. Thanks very much for them all.

How is your charwoman getting on? She sounded too good to be true from your description. I think your suggestion about sending the dock strikers out here is a good one. We used to say the same thing out here about the coal strikers – there are plenty of men out here who would be only too happy to do their jobs at their rates of pay.

I'm glad to hear Uncle Matt is improving now. I'm writing to them when I finish this to acknowledge the films that Aunt Edith sent – they arrived 2 or 3 days ago. I wonder where she gets her weird ideas about M & B tablets? They are excellent drugs, and to my knowledge have no after-effects. I must have seen 10s of thousands of sulphonamide tablets administered out here with nothing but good results.

Thanks for the parcel you have sent me. I hope it arrives safely! It won't arrive for months yet, of course, but I don't mind when it comes as long as it arrives safely. Cigarettes are again short here – the famous NAAFI – you know, goes everywhere the troops go – hasn't been seen here yet, so all we get is a ration (with our grub ration) of 50 Woodbines a week. Even that is only half of our official entitlement. However, I get some from the non-smokers, and to help out, I got 2 duty free parcels from Mam a day or two ago. Not too bad, you will be thinking, Ann, in view of the cigarette shortage at home!

I suppose you'll be wanting some news from me? Well, we are still in Sourabaya, bringing "law and order" to the Indonesians. It is quite simple, our method of "pacifying" a country – we merely blow the town to bits with bombs & shells & kill the inhabitants by thousands until they decide they have had enough. We have 200 odd Javanese civilians in here – legs blown off, arms missing, shot in the guts, head, everywhere – ranging from kids of 2 or 3 months to old men and women of 70 and 80. The laugh of it all is that the country doesn't even belong to us – we kill the Javanese, and the Javanese kill our lads and in the end it's the Dutch who will take over the country, and Britain's name will stink for years out here as the murderer of civilians.

Believe me, my eyes have been opened in the last month. We have fought for 6 years for the rights of small nations, to remove foreign aggression, and for the principle of self-determination, – but these benefits seem only to be conferred upon those whom it suits us – Indians, Indochinese and Indonesians seem to be excluded.

No one here has the slightest interest in the fighting and our one thought is to get out. I now have 2 years 1 month overseas – I hope I keep a whole skin till my 3 years are up.

All for now.

Love, Harry.

The Chinese community in Surabaya, about 10 per cent of the city's population, supported the Allies during the occupation and Harry's letters in December mention their gratitude for the medical care his unit provided. During December, the 5th Division cleared an area around Surabaya and sent patrols out to locate the remaining internees and prisoners still in Indonesian hands. The soldiers of the occupying division lived among civilians, an unusual experience for them, in a damaged and nervous city under curfew.

5.I.M.S.U. S.E.A.C.
15th December 1945

Dear Ann,

I haven't acknowledged your letter of Nov. 21st in which you wished me a merry Xmas, nor even, I think, your previous one of Nov. 12th. So it's about time I bestirred myself and let you know I'm still alive.

Thank you for your Xmas greetings, Annie. Here's a merry Xmas to you, and a happy and prosperous New Year. I am enclosing half of your Xmas present, a pair of silk stockings, one of some which were given to me by a Chinese fellow here. I hope they fit, and that the colour is satisfactory. I can't get the pair into one envelope, as it makes it too bulky. Let's hope they both arrive safely – it will be annoying if only one arrives!

Sourabaya is much quieter now. The Indonesian soldiers have been driven quite a few miles from the city, and the civilians are slowly returning. We have stopped admitting new cases, so we are able to concentrate on operating on the 200 people we have in already. It is expected that we shall be cleared of patients by the new year, so what we will be doing after that, I don't know.

Probably we'll be sent to another trouble centre. I am so fed up with our two faced policy out here, and the fact that we are still in action though the war is over, that I have stopped grumbling, and just resign myself to any rotten thing my dearly beloved country will think up next.

I won't try to write at length in this letter, but will finish it off in the letter with the other stocking.

So cheerio,

Love,

Harry.

Figure 54: The Chinese Red Cross in Surabaya. Bert Hardy, No. 9 Army Film and Photo Section, Army Film and Photographic Unit. (*IWM SE 5641. Reproduced with permission*)

5.I.M.S.U. S.E.A.C.
15th December 1945

Dear Ann,

Here is the 2nd instalment of my letter, and the other half of your pair of stockings.

I was interested in what you said about seeing a film of some island near Singapore to which the Japs were being sent. For that was the island (amongst others) to which I sailed and which I told you about. Sempang is its name.

I had a Xmas card from Les Murchie two days ago. He is still in Malaya, in Serembau, I imagine, as that was the last address I knew.

He is a captain now. Also had a letter from Jack Blackburn. He tells me he is due to go home next November, but he is hoping, now that the war has finished, to get home in May. Lucky man!

I still don't see any speed up in my return, and I expect to reach home about the end of next November. I wonder if demob. will have reached group 46 by then? I doubt it, at the rate the Govt. is fiddling with release just now. But there again, I have pretty well got past the grumbling stage, and am beginning to adopt a passive attitude. You get to the stage when you realise that you are powerless to do anything, and that no amount of grumbling will get you anywhere.

I feel quite depressed at the thought of spending a third Xmas overseas, this one in a much worse climate than either of the other two, and further away from home than ever. The only consolation is that it will probably be my last Xmas away from home, and that I should be able to spend my next one at home. I'll soon be saying "See you sometime this year"! Roll on the days till I get on that boat for England!

Closing now, Ann. Hope you like the stockings. Once more, a merry Xmas to you, and a happy New Year.

Love,
Harry.

5.I.M.S.U. S.E.A.C.
15th December 1945

Dear Flo,

Here is my Xmas letter to you (in 2 instalments) and my Xmas present to you (also in instalments). I got a few pairs of stockings presented to me by a Chinese as a form of thanks for the work we have done for the Chinese casualties in the recent fighting, so don't blame me if they don't fit, or the shade doesn't suit!

I hope they are all right, Flo. Anyway, you know, even if they aren't that the spirit is, anyway! Here's wishing you a very merry Xmas and a happy 1946. Got anything to drink the new year in with? So far we have each 1 bottle of Irish whisky, 1/2 bottle English Gin, 6 tins American beer, 1 port, 1 sherry, 1 hock, 1 burgundy, and 1 white wine! That's only December's ration – Xmas ration isn't in yet! Do I make you envious??

Thanks for your letter of 13th Nov. – I'm afraid I have been very slow in acknowledging it. But we are busy operating every damn day, and practically the only letters I write are the ones to home.

Will finish this off in the other letter.

Love,

Harry.

5.I.M.S.U. S.E.A.C.
15th December 1945

Dear Flo,

Continuing my first letter. We have stopped admitting new cases – that is being done by another field ambulance and surgical unit – but we have 200 old ones to look after. Most of them are civilians, injured in the fighting of last month. We operated on them when they came in, but each day 6 or more of them require plaster casts changed, wounds sutured, or other operative procedures. So we are kept busy.

We are gradually evacuating them to a Dutch civil hospital which has come in, and we are supposed to be empty by the end of the year. What will happen then no-one knows, but we will almost certainly be moved somewhere else as soon as we have no patients to look after.

We all are hoping we shall be moved back to Malaya, but we think that such a move would be too good to be true! In any case, I am certain the trouble in Java won't be over by the end of the year. At the moment it is only the Indonesian extremists who are fighting us, but I see in yesterday's local news sheet that the Prime Minister of the self-styled Indonesian Republic has said that if as a result of the Singapore conference the Allies decide on joint action against Java, then all the Indonesians will rise and fight. And I won't blame them if they do!

We've been fighting for 6 years for freedom, and making grand speeches about it. Well, the Javanese saw their chance to grab their freedom while the Dutch were away, and, by golly, they took it! They would be fools to give it up without a fight. If we want to fight they'll give it to us! Of course we, with superior arms, including aircraft, will win in the end. Just as Germany did against Poland, Denmark, Holland, Norway, Belgium and the rest. Just as Italy did in Abyssinia. There is little to choose between our "mission of law & order" here and the Axis powers' "brutal crushing of free peoples".

But enough of this in a Xmas letter. And I must finish it off by once again wishing you a very merry Xmas, Flo, and may 1946 see me coming round to Newham Avenue again for a bite of supper!

Love,

Harry.

5.I.M.S.U. S.E.A.C.
23rd December 1945

Dear Annie & Flo,

It's almost Xmas now, and to celebrate the event I sent off two days ago a further present to you both – a parcel containing 2 tablecloths and traycloth. I hope my previous presents in the letters arrived safely, as well as the parcel.

Thank you for 3 cards which have arrived recently. 1 from you Ann, today, and one yesterday (4th & 12th Dec.). And one from you Flo, yesterday, written on 6th Dec.

Don't get <u>too</u> worried about me, Ann! I've come through over 18 months of front line service so far – I should be lucky enough to last the rest! <u>I</u> don't worry about myself (at least, when the shells or other missiles aren't coming <u>too</u> near!).

We are just looking forward to Xmas. We are having a quiet Xmas Day – just our own officers in our own mess. On the 27th we are having a party, with a dance, and that, of course, will be much noisier! We only have 4 patients left, and expect to unload them at any time, so we won't be troubled with work over Xmas.

After Xmas we expect to move to a new site at any time, probably about the 28th. It's to a school, and I hear the officers are to have some nice bungalows, so we should be alright. How long we'll be there is another matter – there are all sorts of rumours about future attacks on the Indonesians, but nothing definite.

I had a card yesterday from Uncle Matt. It's good to hear that he's got over what must have been a serious illness.

At the moment it is raining and there is a pleasant cool breeze blowing. This usually happens in the evening, but the rest of the day is sweltering and very sticky. I shall certainly be glad to get out of this plague spot and back to a decent climate.

There's a rumour floating round that all medical officers to group 40 and specialist M.O.s up to group 30 are to be back in U.K. by Jan 31st. Too bad for me – I am group 46 and a specialist at that! So I've had it! Still, it's only a rumour so far, and in any case I should be home in about 10 months anyway.

You asked me some time ago if I had an Indian batman. Have I never told you about my batman Saifan? Pronounced as in whisky?! Or my previous batman Bhajam' Singh? Remind me to tell you about them some day when I come home.

I could just eat some of your fish & chips, Flo, that you were making as Ann wrote her last letter! Maybe it won't be very long before I can.

Closing now.

Love,

Harry.

This is the last of Harry's letters. The 5th Division set up civilian hospitals and an ambulance service, as well as schools, a police force and infrastructure, but there are no letters to say if Harry played a role in rebuilding Surabaya. His New Year snap outside his bungalow, in a jokey pose holding a Japanese sword, appears to contradict his angry letters, maybe to reassure the people back home. Dutch civilian officials arrived in January and Dutch soldiers in February and March. Meanwhile, groups of Japanese were still surrendering. In April 1946, the 5th Division returned to India. Indonesia became independent in 1949.

Harry did not return to India with the division. His father had an incapacitating heart attack, and was to die later in the year and Harry

Figure 55: New Year, 1946. Harry looking thin but surprisingly cheerful outside his bungalow in Surabaya. (*Author's collection*)

was repatriated in March on compassionate grounds, some months earlier than planned. He spent the rest of his military service at the hospital in Catterick Camp in Yorkshire, close to home.

Several of the memoirs written by temporary officers like Harry make a point of saying that their time in the Army forced an evaluation of self, of others and of their role in the world. For Harry, front-line service meant frantic activity punctuated by spells of reflection and exasperation with 'base-wallahs'. When Charles Evans joined his Malaria Forward Treatment Unit 'for the first time in the army I had a sense of belonging, of being one of a unit that was going somewhere with a purpose'. For Paddy Donaldson, 'Up where the bullets were flying there was much more efficiency – a great spirit of co-operation and helpfulness'.

But there were also traumatic experiences that no civilian could imagine and aspects of the conduct of the war which disgusted Harry and led to loss of trust in politicians. He was not alone. About Surabaya, Paddy Donaldson recalled 'with vivid horror, bodies floating through the harbour and out to sea. This depressing sight filled me with doubts. Was this slaughter really necessary? Had we not just celebrated VJ Day? Was this really a good cause? Or was it the unacceptable face of colonialism?'

Overall, the war matured Harry and expanded his horizons. Paddy Donaldson gained 'a completely new perception on life … My life's landscape had forever changed … I now had a clear vision of where I wanted to go in my career.' Harry must have felt the same.

Return Home

Harry wasn't to know it, of course, but on his return he had only 13 years to live. Into it he crammed surgical work at Catterick military hospital, a short period in general practice to familiarise himself with civilian medicine again, and a specialist course in anaesthetics at his *alma mater* in Edinburgh before his appointment as consultant anaesthetist to the Teesside hospitals in the new National Health Service.

He married Margaret, his 'student sweetheart', as the report had it in the local newspaper, and they took over his childhood home in Middlesbrough

Figure 56: Wedding day, October 1946. (*Author's collection*)

Figure 57: The 1950s. Left, the consultant anaesthetist. Right, the sailor. (*Author's collection*)

from his widowed mother. They had three daughters: me, Alison and Elizabeth. He reconnected with his family and friends and returned to civilian activities. Like his father and grandfather he loved the North York Moors and leased a cottage in Rosedale, an isolated farming community at that time without telephone or electricity. He built his own boat in the garage at the bottom of the back garden of the Linthorpe house and sailed it at Runswick Bay. He formed links with Scotland again as a sailing instructor on the Clyde and on family holidays in North Berwick near Edinburgh.

He and Margaret made trips to London for the Boat Show and the Ideal Home Exhibition. The mahogany mantelpieces in the Linthorpe house were removed and Edwardian furniture replaced by the latest Danish designs from Heals. At the time he died, the car was packed ready for his and Margaret's first holiday abroad. In the words of the Prime Minister, the country had 'never had it so good' and the comfortable life his parents had lived beckoned. There were sadnesses. Annie died in 1954 and Harry

Figure 58: Flo with Ginger, about 1950. Kate on right. 21 The Crescent. (*Author's collection*)

Figure 59: Annie on the beach with Alison, about 1951. Margaret on right. (*Author's collection*)

was present when she died. His brother John suffered a fatal heart attack later in the same year, leaving a young widow and two children. But his twin brothers Bob and Jim married and started families, and their joint dental practice flourished. Belinda the beagle replaced Ginger the terrier.

The Burma campaign remained significant for him. In the Linthorpe attics were a bush hat, his medals, and a Japanese sword, flag and kimono, and there were wood carvings from Java on the sitting-room shelves. One of his good friends was imprisoned by the Japanese, the only doctor in a camp in Taiwan,[1] another friend had been a surgeon in Burma, and Harry remained in contact with the commander of the last field ambulance to which his unit had been attached. But I never heard my father talk about the War and I was too young to ask questions. He died of a heart attack on 18 July 1959, a casualty of all those cigarettes.

Envoi

Friends ask, 'the Chindits?', or 'the Burma railway?' if I mention that my father was in the Burma campaign. It is these extreme, unusual experiences that define the campaign in the popular mind. But the campaign was much more complex; it was not all about prison camps and jungle guerilla warfare. Louis Allen has written the most comprehensive historical account and the subtitle of his 1984 book summarises the campaign: *The Longest War, 1941-1945*.[1] It was the longest campaign fought by the British during the War and Allen wrote that 'the war in Burma is not just a magnificent story, it is a whole host of magnificent stories'. There was a humiliating British defeat when the Japanese invaded in 1941; a lengthy fighting retreat to India in 1942 over a thousand miles of difficult country; the rebuilding of a functioning, multi-ethnic, multi-lingual force during 1943; sieges; trench warfare comparable to that of the First World War; hand-to-hand fighting of ancient ferocity; combined operations with air and naval forces; artillery barrages; opposed crossings of great rivers; tank warfare in the Burmese central plain; and the final rapid advance ahead of the monsoon to Rangoon. The letters place the episodes of Harry's war within these 'magnificent stories' and illuminate their small details and minor footnotes.

The history of a war is a bit like the history of an individual and the process of looking for Harry has brought me up against the nature of evidence for not only wars but also for the people who fought in them. What remains of a war are the Cabinet papers, other official documents, the logistical inventories, the command maps with their sweeping arrows. Similarly, the records that survive for most people are the milestone incidents: births, marriages and deaths, court appearances, directory entries, newspaper articles. But there are great stretches of life between the documented events and maybe the unrecorded quotidian is at least as important, the daily changes in the weather, the food, cigarettes and books, the minor illnesses and ritual conversations, the grouses, prejudices and small pleasures.

The letters show this period of Harry's life as he saw it and I look through his eyes when he describes his surroundings. Through his words I can share his exuberance when he is given a jeep to play with, his pleasure at gifts of books and magazines, his horror of snakes, his misery at the prospect of never-ending mud and rain, and his addiction to cigarettes.

In some ways he is straightforward and easy to read but he is also far more complex and paradoxical than I had understood before I read the letters. I realise that I share some of his, often inconsistent, traits. He is articulate and funny but also gloomy. He is liberal-minded and curious about other people but also dismissive, rude and judgmental. He is upset and aggrieved at unfairness and disloyalty and I empathise with the angry helplessness in his letters, his sense that the world should not be like this. I can understand the tensions between wanting to explore new ideas and new lands and wanting to hunker down with familiar places and people. He's hard-working, happiest when he is busy, and inclined to ruminate introspectively when there is no clear plan for the future. He wants a bigger, more benign, state with social reform and welfare but resents the idea of bureaucratic interference in his own professional life. He holds these already contradictory ideas while simultaneously hating jobsworthism, lead-swinging and laziness. He is an agnostic but the moral certainties from generations of chapel-going ancestors are deeply ingrained. He is widely-read and has eclectic tastes but family and home root him. He loves conversation and reading and is also pragmatic and practical.

I feel proud that he is a bookworm, like me, as if I have somehow brought this about. I feel glad that he had people in his life like Annie and Flo, intelligent women who cared about him, and who cared about me too. The correspondence with them created a grounded and familiar world away from mud and blood and awful cigarettes, a world of Middlesbrough and the moors, family and friends, books and talk, where he is a boy again, cycling round to Annie's and Flo's house in Newham Avenue for a fish supper and a 'parliament' round the fire.

Notes

Introduction

1. John Keegan, *The Face of Battle*, London: Cape, 1976.
2. Sigurdur Gylfi Magnusson and Istvan M Szijarto, *What is Microhistory? Theory and Practice*, London: Routledge, 2013.

Joining Up

1. War Office, *190 Field Ambulance*, National Archives: WO 177/788.

India

1. George MacDonald Fraser, *Quartered Safe out Here: A Recollection of the War in Burma with a New Epilogue: Fifty Years On*, London: Harper, 2000.
2. War Office, *21 General Hospital*, National Archives: WO 177/2192.
3. R.J. Donaldson, *Off the Cuff*, Richmond: Murray, 2000.
4. Charles Evans, *A Doctor in XIVth Army: Burma 1944-1945*, London: Leo Cooper, 1998.

A Cushy Job Looking after the Chindits

1. Mountbatten of Burma, *Report to the Combined Chiefs of Staff by the Supreme Allied Commander, South-East Asia, 1943-1945*, London: HMSO, 1951.
2. These memoirs include: Bernard Fergusson, *Beyond the Chindwin* and *The Wild Green Earth*, London: Collins, 1945 and 1946; Michael Calvert, *Prisoners of Hope*, London: Cape, 1952; John Masters, *The Road Past Mandalay*, London: Michael Joseph, 1961.
3. Kevin Blackburn and Karl Hack, *Forgotten Captives in Japanese-Occupied Asia*, London: Routledge, 2008.
4. James H. Stone (ed.), *Crisis Fleeting: Original Reports on Military Medicine in India and Burma in the Second World War*, Washington DC: Office of the Surgeon General, Department of the Army, 1969.
5. Quoted in: Mark Harrison, *Medicine and Victory*, Oxford: Oxford University Press, 2008.

Anaesthetics and the Arakan

1. Mabel was an aunt of Harry's.
2. Airgraph. These were written on a special form that was microfilmed before being sent by air, then developed and printed at the destination.
3. None of the letters written to his family survive.
4. Marion was Harry's sister.
5. Mary was the cousin who preserved these letters.
6. Marion, Mary, and Mary's sister Margaret were working in Bath in administrative roles for the Admiralty.

7. Marion's nickname.
8. Leslie Murchie, a school friend.
9. Jack Blackburn, 'Blackie', was another school friend, married and working in the industrial area in Bengal. Harry later visited him.
10. Eddie Knott, a school friend.

Kohima

1. War Office, *66 Indian General Hospital*, National Archives: WO 177/2234.
2. F.A.E. Crew, *The Army Medical Services: Volume V: Burma*, in *History of the Second World War: United Kingdom Medical Series*, London: HMSO, 1956. Abbreviated here to 'the *Official History*.' Later unattributed quotations come from the same source.
3. Jack Blackburn.
4. The Transporter Bridge over the Tees opened in 1911 with great fanfare and is still an icon of Middlesbrough's skyline.

5th Indian Mobile Surgical Unit

1. War Office, *5 Indian Mobile Surgical Unit*, National Archives: WO 177/2329.
2. War Office, *A Field Surgery Pocket Book*, London: War Office, 1944.
3. John A. Baty, *Surgeon in the Jungle War*, London: Kimber, 1979.
4. Donaldson, *op. cit.*
5. Robert J. Stout, *Records*, Wellcome Library: GC/226/A5.
6. J.A. R[oss], *Memoirs of an Army Surgeon*, Edinburgh: Blackwood, 1948.

Imphal

1. Sir James Grigg, Secretary of State for War in Churchill's Cabinet.
2. Leo Amery, Secretary of State for India.
3. Ginger was Harry's dog.
4. Harry's twin brothers, Bob and Jim, were about to leave school and both planned to become dentists, like their father.

Burma Borderlands

1. Secretaries of State for War and India, Grigg and Amery.
2. Evans, *op. cit.*
3. Aunt Edith was Harry's father's sister and the mother of his cousins Mary and Margaret, two of the 'Bath Belles'.
4. Harry's brother John.
5. Clive Richardson, a school friend.
6. ENSA = Entertainments National Service Association. NAAFI = Navy, Army and Air Force Institutes. Both were set up as welfare organisations for the troops.
7. Matthew Davies, married to Harry's Aunt Edith.
8. The American Field Service ambulance drivers were volunteers who were unfit for regular military service and were much admired by British troops.
9. Margaret, Harry's cousin, who married during the War.

Irrawaddy Shore

1. Kirby School, a girls' Grammar School in Middlesbrough.
2. Geoffrey FitzClarence, 5th Earl of Munster, Under-Secretary of State for the Home Department.
3. *Illustrated London News*.
4. Ernest Hemingway and Theodore Dreiser.
5. Harry's great-aunt.
6. It is unclear why Harry made these flights.
7. Dick Donovan, *The Man from Manchester*, London: Chatto, 1890. He is correct. It is like nineteenth-century melodrama.
8. Predecessor of today's *New Statesman*.
9. *Now* was published by Freedom Press as a forum for controversial writing, 1940-7.

Rangoon

1. *News Review*, a British news magazine published by Cosmopolitan Press, 1936–50.
2. Middlesbrough was the first major British industrial target to be bombed by the Luftwaffe. The first raid was on 25 May 1940.
3. The reference to 'this unit' implies that it may have been possible for individual doctors to opt out of treating Japanese prisoners on grounds of conscience, as is the case for abortions in the UK today.
4. This may have been the perception in the army, but these numbers are inaccurate. There were fewer Japanese deaths than he estimates and more prisoners.
5. Harry's cousin Margaret and her new husband.
6. Beverley Nicholls, *Verdict on India*, London: Cape, 1944.
7. Pagan (or Bagan), a former royal city, now an extensive area scattered with the pink stone ruins of mediaeval pagodas.

Snakes, Cigarettes, and Weddings

1. Richard Doll and Austin Bradford Hill, 'Mortality in Relation to Smoking: Ten Years' Observations of British Doctors', *British Medical Journal* 1964:1;1399-1410.
2. J.L.S. Coulter, *The Royal Naval Medical Service. Volume 1: Administration* and *Volume 2: Operations*, London: HMSO, 1954 and 1956.
3. B.J. Crabb, *Beyond the Call of Duty: The Loss of British Commonwealth Mercantile and Service Women at Sea During the Second World War*, Donington: Shaun Tyas, 2006.
4. Ashley Jackson, *Ceylon at War, 1939-1945*, Warwick: Helion, 2018.
5. Alan Moorehead, *A Year of Battle*, London: Hamish Hamilton, 1943.
6. Geraldine Horton, *No Nightingale Sang*, Hythe: Volturna Press, 1996.
7. Flo was a secretary in a steel plant in Middlesbrough.
8. Possibly the Burmese Liberation Army, led by Aung San, initially in collaboration with the Japanese. It was re-named the Burma Defence Army in 1943, defected to the Allies in March 1945, and was re-named the Patriotic Burmese Forces in June 1945.

Singapore

1. Cambodia, Vietnam and Laos.
2. Indonesia.

3. Composite, or 'compo' rations were designed to bridge the gap before army cooks set up established cooking and mess facilities. The tins and packets came in crates containing food for fourteen men and were cooked up by individual sections themselves.
4. Jack O'Hara. He was a contemporary of Harry's at medical school. He was mentioned in despatches, and after the War became a general practitioner in Rotherham.

Return Home

1. Katherine M. Venables, 'Captain George Blair RAMC: A Doctor Prisoner of the Japanese in Singapore and Taiwan in the Second World War', *Journal of Medical Biography* 2025;33:93-105.

Envoi

1. Louis Allen, *Burma: The Longest War 1941-45*, London: Dent, 1984.

Timeline

1890	Annie born
1893	Flo born
1914	First World War begins
1915	Harry Walker Senior and Edith Evans marry in Middlesbrough
1918	Harry born Armistice Day and the First World War ends
1920	John (brother) born
1921	Marion (sister) born
1927	Twins James and Robert (brothers) born
1935	Leaves Middlesbrough High School for medical school in Edinburgh
1936	Spanish Civil War begins
1939	Britain declares war on Germany Starts the clinical part of the medical course in Edinburgh
1940	Student nurse Margaret Wallace becomes his girlfriend
1942	Starts work as a house officer in the North Riding Infirmary Graduates Margaret Wallace joins QARNNS
13.03.43	Joins RAMC as lieutenant and posted to No. 1 Depot, Crookham
12.04.43	Posted to 190 Field Ambulance, Northern Ireland, for training
29.08.43	Tropical medicine course, Liverpool
09.43	Embarkation leave in Middlesbrough, proposes to Margaret Wallace
10–11.43	*Strathmore* leaves Liverpool in convoy, is attacked in Mediterranean, and arrives in Bombay
02.12.43	Posted to 21 British General Hospital, Jhansi
05.12.43	First letter to 'Dear Annie & Flo'
09.03.44	Anaesthetics course, 133 Indian and British General Hospital, Bareilly
03.44	Promoted captain Japanese Operation U-Go begins, the 'March on Delhi' Kohima encircled
04.44	Kohima casualties evacuated Seconded to 66 Indian General Hospital, Dimapur, for Kohima casualties Hospitalised with dysentery Visits Delhi Margaret Wallace posted to Ceylon

31.05.44	Posted to 5 Indian Mobile Surgical Unit, Palel, Imphal Unit transfers from 20th Division to 5th Division
06.44	D-Day landings in Europe Allies open Kohima-Imphal road
07.44	Japanese retreat from Imphal into the mountainous Burmese borderlands
08.44	Allies fight down the Tiddim Road
09.44	Crossing of the Manipur River
10.44	Unit still in mountains. Many Japanese corpses. Unit transfers from 5th Division to 17th Division
11.44	Kalemyo entered
12.44	Unit transfers from 17th Division to 2nd Division Crossing of the Chindwin River
01.45	Shwebo plain
02.45	Crossing of the Irrawaddy River
03.45	Mandalay taken
04.45	Unit transfers from 2nd Division to 17th Division Based at Pegu near Waw
05.45	Rangoon taken VE Day, the end of the war in Europe Unit transfers from 17th Division to 5th Division
07.45	Month's leave in Darjeeling and Burnpur
08.45	A-bombs dropped on Hiroshima and Nagasaki VJ Day, the initial Japanese surrender
09.45	Unit moves on *Dilwarra* to Singapore Formal Japanese surrender
11.45	Unit moves on *Dilwarra* to Surabaya, Java
12.45	Final letter to 'Dear Annie & Flo'
1946	Repatriated and posted to Catterick Camp Hospital Marries Margaret Wallace Harry Senior dies
1947	Advanced anaesthetics course, Royal Infirmary, Edinburgh Released from military service as Major Walker
1948	Consultant appointment, Teesside group of hospitals Katherine (daughter) born
1950	Alison (daughter) born
1951	Takes Rosedale cottage
1954	Elizabeth (daughter) born Annie dies John (brother) dies
1959	Harry dies Family live temporarily with Flo before moving to new house
1967	Katherine (daughter) starts medical school
1968	Flo dies

Bibliography

Allen, Louis, *Burma: The Longest War 1941–45*, London: Dent, 1984.

Baty, John A., *Surgeon in the Jungle War*, London: Kimber, 1979.

Blackburn, Kevin and Karl Hack (eds), *Forgotten Captives in Japanese-Occupied Asia*, London: Routledge, 2007.

Blair, George, *Capt George Blair, RAMC*, Wellcome Library: PP/GBL.

Calvert, Michael, *Prisoners of Hope*, London: Cape, 1952.

Childers, Erskine, *The Riddle of the Sands: A Record of Secret Service*, Oxford: Sidgwick & Jackson, 1931. First published London: Nelson's Library, 1903.

Cohen, Jack, *Administrative Notes for Royal Army Medical Corps Officers*, Aldershot: Gale & Polden, 1941.

Coulter, J.L.S., *The Royal Naval Medical Service. Volume 1: Administration*, in *History of the Second World War: United Kingdom Medical Series*, London: HMSO, 1954.

Coulter, J.L.S., *The Royal Naval Medical Service. Volume 2: Operations*, in *History of the Second World War: United Kingdom Medical Series*, London: HMSO, 1956.

Crabb, B.J., *Beyond the Call of Duty: The Loss of British Commonwealth Mercantile and Service Women at Sea During the Second World War*, Donington: Shaun Tyas, 2006.

Crew, F.A.E., *The Army Medical Services: Volume I: Administration*, in *History of the Second World War: United Kingdom Medical Series*, London: HMSO, 1953.

Crew, F.A.E., *The Army Medical Services: Volume V: Burma*, in *History of the Second World War: United Kingdom Medical Series*, London: HMSO, 1956.

Doll, Richard and Austin Bradford Hill, 'Mortality in Relation to Smoking: Ten Years' Observations of British Doctors', *British Medical Journal* 1964:1;1399–1410.

Donaldson, R.J., *Off the Cuff*, Richmond: Murray, 2000.

Donovan, Dick, *The Man from Manchester*, London: Chatto, 1890.

Dreiser, Theodore, *An American Tragedy*, London: Constable, 1926.

Evans, Charles, *A Doctor in XIVth Army: Burma 1944-1945*, London: Leo Cooper, 1998.

Fergusson, Bernard, *Beyond the Chindwin*, London: Collins, 1945.

Fergusson, Bernard, *The Wild Green Earth*, London: Collins, 1946.

Fraser, George MacDonald, *Quartered Safe out Here: A Recollection of the War in Burma with a New Epilogue: Fifty Years On*, London: Harper, 2000.

Harrison, Mark, *Medicine and Victory*, Oxford: Oxford University Press, 2008.

Hemingway, Ernest, *Fiesta*, London: Jonathan Cape, 1927.

Horton, Geraldine, *No Nightingale Sang*, Hythe: Volturna Press, 1996.

Jackson, Ashley, *Ceylon at War, 1939-1945*, Warwick: Helion, 2018.

Keegan, John, *The Face of Battle*, London: Cape, 1976.

Lawrence, T.E., *Seven Pillars of Wisdom: a Triumph*, London: Cape, 1935.

Magnusson, Sigurdur Gylfi, and Istvan M. Szijarto, *What is Microhistory? Theory and Practice*, London: Routledge, 2013.
Masters, John, *The Road Past Mandalay*, London: Michael Joseph, 1961.
Moorehead, Alan, *A Year of Battle*, London: Hamish Hamilton, 1943.
Mountbatten of Burma, *Report to the Combined Chiefs of Staff by the Supreme Allied Commander, South-East Asia, 1943-1945*, London: HMSO, 1951.
Nehru, Jawaharlal, *An Autobiography: With Musings on Recent Events in India*, London: John Lane, 1936.
Nehru, Jawaharlal, *Glimpses of World History: Being Further Letters to His Daughter, Written in Prison, and Containing a Rambling Account of History for Young People*, London: Drummond, 1939.
Newhouse, Muriel, *Dr Muriel "Molly" Newhouse (1912-2000), FRCP, FFOM: Memoir of Service in the RAMC During World War Two*, Wellcome Library: MS.8766.
Nicholls, Beverley, *Verdict on India*, London: Cape, 1944.
Ransome, Arthur, *Swallows and Amazons*, London: Cape, 1930.
R[oss], J.A., *Memoirs of an Army Surgeon*, Edinburgh: Blackwood, 1948.
Stone, James H. (ed.), *Crisis Fleeting: Original Reports on Military Medicine in India and Burma in the Second World War*, Washington DC: Office of the Surgeon General, Department of the Army, 1969.
Stout, Robert J., *Records of Anaesthesia for Surgical Operations*, Wellcome Library: GC/226/A5.
Tuller, Theodore, *Letters Home from Medical School*, Royal College of Surgeons Edinburgh: GD 83.
Venables, Katherine M., 'Captain George Blair RAMC: A Doctor Prisoner of the Japanese in Singapore and Taiwan in the Second World War', *Journal of Medical Biography* 2025;33:93-105.
War Office, *A Field Surgery Pocket Book: Memoranda Mainly Based on Experience in the Present War*, London: War Office, 1944.
War Office, *7 Malaria Forward Treatment Unit*, National Archives: WO 177/2025.
War Office, *190 Field Ambulance*, National Archives: WO 177/788.
War Office, *21 British General Hospital*, National Archives: WO 177/2192.
War Office, *66 Indian General Hospital*, National Archives: WO 177/2234.
War Office, *5 Indian Mobile Surgical Unit*, National Archives: WO 177/2329.
War Office, *Prisoners of war, Far East: photographs of POW camp survivors in Rangoon, Saigon, Java and New Guinea; aerial photographs of POW camps in Singapore and Malaya*, National Archives: WO 361/2045.

Further Reading

For Harry's war, the Imperial War Museum has an online database of original photographs and recordings of witness testimony. The National Army Museum and Australian War Memorial have similar, smaller collections. The British Pathé archive contains, as well as photographs, short films shot during the Burma campaign and the BBC website hosts personal accounts by veterans. The Burma Star Association has personal stories in its archive and has created a DVD based on original video and audio recordings. The Museum of Military Medicine's collections can be visited.

Australian War Memorial. www.awm.gov.au.

BBC. *WW2 People's War*. www.bbc.co.uk/history/ww2peopleswar.

British Pathé and Reuters historical collection. www.britishpathe.com.

Burma Star Association. www.burmastar.org.uk and *Burma: 1941–1945*. Leading Edge. Simply Home Entertainment, 2010.

Imperial War Museum collections. www.iwm.org.uk/collections.

Museum of Military Medicine. www.museumofmilitarymedicine.org.uk.

National Army Museum. www.nam.ac.uk.

In addition to the official histories listed in the Bibliography, there are other relevant volumes in the UK series, and the Indian official histories also contain much information relevant to the Burma campaign. I have published an article about battlefield surgery and its memoirs. Frances Houghton provides a historian's perspective on veterans' memoirs. The home front is evoked in *Nella Last's War*.

Houghton, Frances, *The Veterans' Tale: British Military Memoirs of the Second World War*, Cambridge: Cambridge University Press, 2019.

Last, Nella, Richard Broad (ed.) and Suzie Fleming (ed.), *Nella Last's War: The Second World War Diaries of Housewife, 49*, London: Profile, 2006.

MacNalty, A.S. and Mellor, W.F., *Medical Services in War: The Principal Medical Lessons of the Second World War: Based on the Official Medical Histories of the United Kingdom, Canada, Australia, New Zealand and India*, London: HMSO, 1968.

Mellor, W.F., *History of the Second World War: Casualties and Medical Statistics*, London: HMSO, 1972.

Raina, B.L., *Administration*, Delhi: Combined Inter-Services Historical Section, India and Pakistan, 1953.

Raina, B.L., *Medicine, Surgery and Pathology*, Delhi: Combined Inter-Services Historical Section, India and Pakistan, 1955.

Raina, B.L., *The Campaigns in the Eastern Theatre*, Delhi: Combined Inter-Services Historical Section, India and Pakistan, 1964.
Raina, B.L., *World War II: Medical Services, India*, New Delhi: Commonwealth Publishers, 1990.
Venables, Katherine M., 'Surgery on the Battlefield: Mobile Surgical Units in the Second World War and the Memoirs They Produced', *Journal of Medical Biography* 2023:31;202-11.

For the Middlesbrough where Harry was born, Florence Bell's *At the Works* was a pioneering social study of the town at the time when Harry's father was a child, and the town was the subject of sociological investigation again towards the end of the War, described in Ruth Glass' *Social Background of a Plan*. Asa Briggs included Middlesbrough in his survey of Victorian cities. Later, Beynon, Hudson and Sadler, and Yasumoto outlined the town's unique history.

Bell, Florence Eveleen Eleanore Olliffe, *At the Works: A Study of a Manufacturing Town*, London: Edward Arnold, 1907. Reprinted, London: Virago, 1985.
Beynon, Huw, Ray Hudson and David Sadler, *A Place Called Teesside: A Locality in a Global Economy*, Edinburgh: Edinburgh University Press for the University of Durham, 1994.
Briggs, Asa, *Victorian Cities*, Harmondsworth: Penguin, 1968.
Glass, Ruth, *The Social Background of a Plan: A Study of Middlesbrough*, London: Routledge & Kegan Paul, 1948.
Yasumoto, Minoru, *The Rise of a Victorian Ironopolis: Middlesbrough and Regional Industrialisation* Woodbridge: Boydell, 2011.

The first two books of David Kynaston's trilogy about the social history of post-war Britain cover the world Harry to which returned.

Kynaston, David, *Austerity Britain, 1945-51*, London: Bloomsbury, 2008.
Kynaston, David, *Family Britain, 1951-57*, London: Bloomsbury, 2010.

Index